2010: The Best
Women's Stage Monologues and Scenes

Edited and with a Foreword
by Lawrence Harbison

MONOLOGUE AND SCENE STUDY SERIES

A SMITH AND KRAUS BOOK
HANOVER, NEW HAMPSHIRE

SMITHANDKRAUS.COM

Published by Smith and Kraus, Inc.
177 Lyme Road, Hanover, NH 03755
SmithandKraus.com

First Edition: September 2010
10 9 8 7 6 5 4 3 2 1

Cover design by Dan Mehling, dmehling@gmail.com
Book design and production by Julia Hill Gignoux,
Freedom Hill Design and Book Production

The Scene Study Series 1067-3253
ISBN-13 978-1-57525-774-7 / ISBN-10 1-57525-774-2
Library of Congress Control Number: 2010931856

NOTE: These scenes are intended to be used for audition and class study; permission is not required to use the material for those purposes. However, if there is a paid performance of any of the scenes included in this book, please refer to Rights and Permissions pages 187–193 to locate the source that can grant permission for public performance.

CONTENTS

SCENES

Foreword

This year Smith and Kraus Publishers has again combined its annual best monologues and best scenes anthologies. Here, you will find a rich and varied selection of monologues and scenes from plays that were produced and/or published in the 2009–2010 theatrical season. Most are for younger performers (teens through thirties), but there are also some excellent pieces for men in their forties and fifties, and even a few for older performers. Some are comic (laughs), some are dramatic (generally, no laughs). Some are rather short, some are rather long. All represent the best in contemporary playwriting.

Several of the monologues are by playwrights whose work may be familiar to you, such as Don Nigro, Theresa Rebeck, Romulus Linney, David Ives, Edward Allan Baker, Arthur Giron, Sarah Ruhl, and Neil LaBute; others are by exciting up-and-comers, such as Cusi Cram, Liz Duffy Adams, Shawn Nacol, and Christine Evans. The scenes are by master playwrights such as Don Nigro, Theresa Rebeck, and Christopher Durang, and by exciting new writers, such as Qui Nguyen, Maura Campbell, Henry Meyerson, Geoffrey Nauffts, and Daniel Talbot. All are representative of the best of contemporary writing for the stage.

Most of the plays from which these monologues have been culled have been published and, hence, are readily available either from the publisher, licensor, or a theatrical bookstore such as Drama Book Shop in New York. A few plays may not be published for a while, in which case contact the author or his or her agent to request a copy of the entire text of the play that contains the monologue that suits your fancy. Information on publishers and rights holders may be found in the rights and permissions section in the back of this anthology.

Break a leg in that audition! Knock 'em dead in class!

Lawrence Harbison
Brooklyn, New York

MONOLOGUES

ALL ABOARD THE MARRIAGE HEARSE

Matt Morillo

Dramatic
Amy, twenty-eight

Amy is speaking to her long-term, live-in boyfriend, Sean. They have just had a fight that has seemingly ended their relationship because of his refusal to get married. Sean has just accused Amy of leaving in anger, and she is trying to explain that she's not leaving out of anger, but that the changes she's gone through have led her to an informed and mature choice.

AMY: All my life, I believed in the fairy tale of "the one." Every guy I've ever dated I wondered, "Is it him? Is it him?" And I made myself sick over it and I probably drove everyone one of those guys crazy . . . Let me finish. But it wasn't until last night that I realized, how cynical that idea is. How cynical is it to suggest that in a world of six billion people, there is only one person that can make you happy? How silly is that? And how crazy do we all make ourselves wondering about that? How much extra unnecessary pressure does that put on relationships? Then we feel this inclination to commit our entire lives to this person because we foolishly believe that they are the only one that could ever make us happy. Well, I'm no longer going to be a slave to that train of thought. So with the next guy I date, I won't put that pressure on him or myself. I'll just live day by day and whatever happens, happens. Perhaps there is no such thing as "the one." Just the one right now.

. . . We were each the one for the past two years and nine months, until last night. But stop interrupting me because I'm trying to thank you. Thanks to you, this breakup is going to be much easier to take for me. I won't get absorbed in the drama of it all. I'll do my crying, and move on to the next guy. Now please give me my phone.

ALL ABOARD THE MARRIAGE HEARSE
Matt Morillo

Dramatic
Amy, twenty-eight

> *Amy is speaking to her long-term, live-in boyfriend, Sean. They have
> just had a fight that has seemingly ended their relationship because of
> his refusal to get married. After Sean tries to convince Amy to stay be-
> cause they are finally thinking on a similar level, she reads one of his old
> columns to him to show him how difficult it's been to live with a cynic
> like him and how different they still are.*

AMY: It's your "Marriage Hearse" column. . . .

You say, "There's a conspiracy here. The government dangles tax
breaks and health benefits in order to entice people to get married. And
why? Because they know marriage is otherwise a dead issue. They are
keeping it alive. No wonder they don't want to give us universal health
care. If they did, then they would lose the only real reason people have
anymore to get married. You see, this keeps the religious nuts happy.
And it all makes sense when you think about it, doesn't it? Marriage and
religion are infinitely similar and they go hand in hand. Religion is a feeble man-made attempt to try and understand something man was never
meant to understand: God. Marriage is a feeble man-made attempt to
try and understand something man was never meant to understand:
Love" . . .

I'm not done, or should I say you're not done. You get cynical several paragraphs later. You say, "Marriage is like a life-support machine.
Life-support machines are man-made mechanisms that prolong a life-
like state for a person who is for all intents and purposes dead. It just
keeps them alive, suffering. Marriage licenses are no different. They are
man-made mechanisms that keep a relationships that is dead, alive, caus-
ing the two people to suffer." . . .

And of course, who can forget your conclusion, "As long as divorce,
prenuptial agreements and adultery exist, and they do in spades,

marriage means nothing and we all know it, so why can't we just all move on from this childish nonsense?" Very nice . . .

And there is actually one question I've always had for you about this column. Why did you open it with this lame quote, "In the words of William Blake, 'But most thro' midnight streets I hear How the youthful Harlots curse. Blasts the new-born Infant's tear. And blights with plagues the marriage hearse.'" Why did you quote that poem? . . .

I looked it up. You know that it's about hookers and venereal disease. It doesn't even make sense in your argument . . .

I don't understand why people call you a humorist.

You're really not that funny.

THE AMISH PROJECT
Jessica Dickey

Seriocomic
Velda, ten to twelve

> *This one-woman play is inspired by a hostage-taking incident that hap-*
> *pened at an Amish school in Lancaster County, Pennsylvania, in October*
> *2006, when five schoolgirls were killed by a gunman. Here, Velda, an*
> *Amish girl, talks to the audience about the same sorts of dreams and fan-*
> *tasies that any girl might have. Later, Velda will die when a crazed man*
> *enters her school and shoots the children.*

VELDA: Soon will be Anna's Rumspringa.
> That's when she has to decide whether or not to join the Church.
> Some don't, but most do, and
> If they don't, we don't speak to them.
> During Anna's Rumspringa
> She's allowed to wear makeup and say cuss words and kiss boys.
> And she can't get in trouble for it.
> I ask Anna everyday if she'll go far away for Rumspringa and she
says she won't,
> but I'm not sure.
> For my Rumspringa I'm going to go to the beach because
> I'm going to wear a bathing suit.
> A red one with flowers on it.
> It will show my breasts a little
> but not too much.
> And a boy will fall in love with me and I'll let him kiss me.
> And eventually, like after a month, the boy will ask me to marry
him, and I'll say, "I can't marry you because you're not Amish." And he'll
say, "Oh please please please!" and I'll say "No no no." And he'll say "Oh
please please please!" and I'll say
> "OK, but you have to become Amish," and he'll say "OK."
> So then I'll bring him home to meet my family and my friends
> and he'll play with my brothers
> and he'll meet Anna (but he won't talk to her that much),
> and then he'll become Amish.

THE AMISH PROJECT

Jessica Dickey

Seriocomic
America, late teens to early twenties

> *America is a waitress in an Amish community that has recently experi-*
> *enced a terrible tragedy: a man entered a school and gunned down the*
> *children in it.*

AMERICA: I work here at the Giant Food on Route 30,
That's how I know the crazy guy's wife.

OK, I know what you're thinking.
You're thinking,
She don't belong here!
Am I right?
You're thinking,
Oh, there are other "other people" in Lancaster besides the Amish?

The answer is yeah.
My mother is Puerto Rican
And I was born here.

She got pregnant with me
as soon as she got here and
That's why she named me
America.
She was two years older than me
when she got pregnant.
I'm sixteen.
OK
I know what you're thinking —
Sixteen and pregnant!
She's a slut.
Am I right?
That's what my mother said:

She said,
I don't work at a filthy chicken factory
Everyday for sixteen years
so my daughter can be a cliché.

OK, she read that word in her *Reader's Digest*, I know it.
I said, Don't quote your Reader's Crygest to me.
My father was some black guy she dated in New York
and then he dumped her when she got pregnant.
But Demetrius
is the only one I ever been with,
So I can't be a slut.

OK,
I know what you're thinking
Demetrius like in *A Midsummer's Night Dream*!
Am I right?!!
We read that play in English this year,
by Mr. William Shakespeare.
I played Titania.
Titania is totally fierce!
She's like, all beautiful and sassy,
And she's got her man but she's still independent.
It was good casting.
I'm thinking about doing my Titania speech for
The Mother-Daughter night at school next month.
You're supposed to have something memorized to recite.

Demetrius and I might get married but I don't know.
We haven't figured that out yet.
He AIN'T gonna dump me.
OK,
I know it's a sin.
I'm a Catholic.
Wait — is it a cliché if I'm a Catholic?
I don't even care cuz if you saw Demetrius
you would understand.
He's got these big lips
that he licks all the time.

He makes me crazy!
I'm like
Demetrius you lickin' those lips
and makin' me crazy!
He just laughs and slaps my butt.

OK, I know you're thinking,
Oh, her and Demetrius gonna have her baby
and live off her mother's minimum wage, but I ain't.
I got a job.
I work here at the Giant Food on Route 30.

(She looks at her belly.)
Nobody can tell yet. I just look like
I had a lot of lasagna.

Telling my mother was the worst.
Last night
We was picking out our outfits
for the Mother-Daughter night at school.
She was digging through the closet
and I told her.
She slapped my face.
She said I'd better look to Saint Francis now,
Only Saint Francis would help me.
Fuck her.

THE AMISH PROJECT
Jessica Dickey

Dramatic
Carol, thirties

> *Carol's husband, Eddie, went crazy and gunned down a group of Amish*
> *schoolchildren in their school. Here, she talks about her life after this*
> *tragedy.*

CAROL: I asked him how they were,
how his little girls were . . .
And he looked at me and said
We must trust in God now.
Is that right?
Trust in God.

I love that.
I love when people say that shit.
Have you turned on the TV lately?
Oh you haven't?
You don't believe in TV?
Well isn't that nice for you.
Lemme fill you in:
shit like this happens every day.
Shit
that is this sick
and more,
happens every fuckin' day.
And the scary thing is,
as mortified as I am by my husband's actions —
the man that I stood before all my friends
and family
and swore to go through my life as ONE —
as disgusting —
Eddie wasn't a bad guy.
He wasn't the Devil.

He just couldn't keep his darkness down anymore,
and it ate him up.
It ate him and it ate those poor little girls,
and now it's eating me.
And you can pull your hat down and say
that's Evil
but the reality is that's all of us.
That's the world.
We're all just a few bad days from SICKO
and that's not Satan, that's the truth.
It lives in me
and yes, it lives in you.

THE AMISH PROJECT
Jessica Dickey

Dramatic
Carol, thirties

> *Carol's husband, Eddie, went crazy and gunned down a group of Amish*
> *schoolchildren in their school. Here, she talks about her confusion and*
> *her guilt when a group of parents of the dead children come to her house*
> *to console her.*

CAROL: Where was your God
when my husband took three guns,
KY Jelly
and plastic ties
and drove over to Stultz Road?

You know you show up here, try to make nice with the Sicko's wife
Well now you know.
Now you see what I am. You can leave.

Amish people putting food in my fridge,
That poor girl at the store tried to help me and
I was such a fuckin' bitch to her.
I wanted to rip my skin off.
I said YOU CAN GET OUT!

And then —
right then — he looks at me.
He looks right at me,
with his weird beard
and his blue eyes,
and there — right there,
in the middle of his eyebrows,
is a Word.
One Word.
And he pushes that Word
into my brain
with his blue stare.

You would think if you're a lowly sack of shit
it'd be pretty great to have an angel
sit in your living room.
Not so much.

To feel like your whole being
is a rotting grave,
and have this
man flower
sit with you,
BE with you . . .
hurts.
It hurts so much.
But it also helps.
In a way that nothing else —

And the Word,
that word . . .
It's like he burned it there,
burned it with his face
into my face.
That Word repeats itself
over and over in my mind.

Every night,
after I put the boys to bed,
I drive over to Stultz Road.
I park the car at the end of the dirt lane
walk the quarter mile to his yard,
and stand before his door,
feeling him on the other side.
The house is usually dark,
they go to bed so much earlier than we do,
but sometimes I see him in there,
see him burdened by the sadness of the world . . .
And then I go home.
I go back to bed.
And the next day is easier.
Easier because —
he exists.

AND SOPHIE COMES TOO
Meryl Cohn

More information on this author may be found on the "Meet the Authors" web page at www.smithandkraus.com.

Dramatic
Ray, thirties

> *Ray is the youngest of the Abramowitz siblings — a boyish androgynous short-haired woman with bound breasts. She is sitting in a chair next to a hospital bed, talking to her mother, who does not stir.*

RAY: Mom, I know you can't answer me, but I think you're in there somewhere, so I don't think it's crazy to talk to you. I mean, people go to *cemeteries* and talk. Now *that's* fucking crazy. If anything remains after someone's dead, it's not in a box in the ground. It's like in the *ether* or something, so if you're going to talk to them, you may as well do it in the shower. So . . . I'm going to tell you, even if Barbara thinks it will upset you. I think you can handle it: I'm leaving for a while. And when I come back from Italy, I'm going to be different. I mean, I'll still be me, but not who you think I am. But I'm not who you think I am now anyway, so maybe it won't be so different. You always wanted a son anyway. If you'll have me, I'll be your son. I don't know if you'll be able to accept it. The biggest problem, if I know you, is what other people will think. But maybe you can figure it out, or maybe we can help you think of what to say about it. Patricia is cool with it. She was all bent out of shape for a while about what it would do to *her* identity, like whether or not she could still be a lesbian and all that. I know you hate that word, but you're lying there looking so peaceful that I just feel like I can say anything: *Lesbian. Gender-fuck. Butt plug.* See, nothing gets a rise out of you anymore. Anyway, Patricia is staying. It doesn't change who she is. It just changes who she loves. I'm not asking for your blessing, because I know that's too much to ask. I'm just asking you not to hate me, OK? I don't think I can handle it if you cut me off, like you did when I was twelve, the first time I said that I felt like I was really a boy. And like a month later, when you still wouldn't talk to me and you looked right past me at the kitchen table, I finally said that I'd made it up to get attention. You put some extra noodle pudding on my plate, and you held my hand for a few seconds. You were so willing to believe that it wasn't true, that I'd made it all up, and I felt so relieved to have you look at me again that I made myself stop thinking about it for a while. I tried to feel like a girl. I don't need you to be happy for me. But I just want you to let me into your house. Like, can I still sit at the table? I still want to be a part of things. I want you to still be my mother.

BARRIO HOLLYWOOD
Elaine Romero

Dramatic
Graciela Moreno, twenty-nine

Graciela is a Latina ballet folklórico dancer. After her younger brother, Alex, receives a brutal head injury while boxing, the doctors conclude he will not recover. Unexpectedly, Alex dies, and the police suspect that his mother has mercy-killed him. Here, the police are interrogating Graciela to find out what she knows about the possible murder.

GRACIELA: We all wanted to believe. See, where I come from, if you have faith, God has pity on you and makes things better. It's like He reaches His hand into your head and captures whatever picture you hold there. And if you imagine it just right, He'll set his hand down on earth and set that picture free. He makes it real. But you've got to believe. That's the first rule of faith. I told my mother we could imagine Alex healthy. Just like she taught me. We would create this powerful image of him. I could see him right there. So beautiful. *(Beat, frustrated.)* I don't know where it went. Has that ever happened to you? Someone you love dies and you just can't see them anymore? *(Beat.)* My mother? She does what she wants. *(Realizing she's incriminated Amá.)* Well, she wants the best for us. Me and Alex. That's all I meant. *(Graciela offers her hands.)* Here. Why don't you arrest me instead? I love my Amá. I'd do anything for her, so go ahead. You found her. At Saint Augustine's Cathedral downtown. Well, it was Sunday morning. Before four a.m.? Please. Have pity on her. My mother's practically a *viejita. (Short beat.)* Well, we get old fast *en mi barrio. (Beat.)* Her going to confession doesn't mean a thing. She goes every week. She always thinks she's got some great sin. She went to confession for breaking the garbage disposal. She went to confession for cheating at poker. She went to confession for taking God's name in vain the day Alex fell in the ring. But who should be confessing here? Maybe God, himself, should go to confession for taking His sword and piercing it straight through my mother's heart?

BARRIO HOLLYWOOD
Elaine Romero

Dramatic
Amá, forty-eight

*Amá is, inside, a little girl who never grew up and who has a difficult
time facing things. She is Graciela and Alex's mother. After her twenty-
four-year-old son Alex receives a brutal head injury while boxing, the
doctors conclude he will not recover. Unexpectedly, Alex dies, and the
police suspect that she has mercy-killed him. In this scene, the police in-
terrogate Amá in an attempt to persuade her to confess to the murder.*

AMA: My son. My child is dead. And you blame me? He killed him. He took
his throat in his hands and he killed him. I saw the whole thing. That
horrible man murdered my son. I am a witness! I want that man to go
to the electric chair! I want him dead! Let him feel what it feels like to
be murdered. *(More upset.)* My son was going to be fine. He had a difficult few months, but he was going to be fine. *(Short beat.)* I did not
sneak off. I went out for some air. *(Short beat.)* No, I did not know he
was dead when I left. I had no idea until you said it to me. What do you
mean — contradicting myself? *(Beat.)* No, I do not have a lawyer. You'll
give me a public defender. All right. You already have ideas in your head.
I can see them floating around in there. I can see that! Maybe I didn't go
to school. Maybe my English is not perfect like yours, but I can see this.
This is not right. *(Short beat.)* I saw everything. Don't pretend. When
you know. *(Breaking down.)* The truth. Let me see Graciela. She knows
why this happened. She knows what kind of slime she let crawl into her
bed. And he calls himself a doctor. *(To herself.)* Taking me from my
church. From my prayers. When my God comforts me. That's who I
love. That's who I listen to. *El siempre está conmigo.* You and your fancy
cars. You and your guns. You've never done nothing good for me. *(Short
beat; yelling to someone as if he's leaving.)* Give me back my suitcase! My
son gave me that. *Para mis cumpleaños.* For my birthday trip. He's giving it to me as a gift. When Graciela turns thirty, I turn forty-eigh. Only
two days apart. *(Getting emotional.)* I saw that pretty island on Channel
52. I saw it in Spanich. It was a beautiful place with canaries up in the

trees. And water — bluer than your eyes. You can see little canaries there like lizards in the desert. Singing all the time. Making everybody happy. And everybody could be happy if some people, some young doctors let God do His job. *(Amá starts crying.)* Simple things. That's all I ever wanted. *(Short beat.)* I didn't kill Alex with my hands but by wanting so much. And he wanted so much to give me those things. He fought when he was bleeding. When he couldn't see. He fought for money. But I kept wanting more. And you know how God feels about that! You must accept what He gives you. And smile. BECAUSE THAT IS HOW GOD WORKS! He makes the rules. He decides. And you take it. Whatever hand you're dealt. But you gotta keep your poker face on. You gotta look like you're winning or you lose that much more. My grandfather taught me that. He was a poker player from Chihuahua. He knew how to fool people into believing him. *(Quickly.)* That's not what I meant.

BEAUTY ON THE VINE

Zak Berkman

More information on this author may be found on the "Meet the Authors" web page at www.smithandkraus.com.

Dramatic
Lauren, early twenties

> *Lauren Chickering was a fast-rising star in right-wing radio capturing the attention of the Hannah Montana generation who normally never listen to talk radio. She was murdered before she could implement her plan to spark a new kind of subversive feminism that taps libertarian passions against big government and big religion. Her radio station broadcasts* The Best of Lauren Chickering *to capitalize on her fame. Here, she is speaking to the listeners of the* Lauren Chickering Radio Show.

LAUREN: I was at the grocery store and a fat woman walked by me. Very fat with a bad dye job, black spandex jogging shorts, too much eye shadow — and she wore a red T-shirt with big lettering that said "All American Mom." No irony. She was mad proud of being who she was: fat, ugly, poorly dressed. There are a lot of these people in our country. Thinking it's OK to be lazy and stupid. How did we get this way? . . . Have we been so brainwashed by the liberal elite telling us we're all equal — that we think it's OK now to be fat slobs? It's this kind of thinking that's destroying America — all these do-gooders on the Left, with their arsenal of guilt trips and obsessions with empathy — they've taken away the meaning of greatness. They've made the mediocre and even the evil . . . acceptable. But they're wrong. We're *not* all equal. We're not all the same. . . . Those poor and disenfranchised suicide bombers are *still* terrorists. Those child-abused serial killers on death row are *still* murderers. And that fat mom is *still* going to die of heart disease or diabetes when she's fifty, leaving her kids with a legacy of resentment and medical bills. Empathy is useless. Some of us *are* better. Am I right? . . . Call me.

BEAUTY ON THE VINE
Zak Berkman

Dramatic
Lauren, early twenties

> *Lauren and her future husband, Sweet, have a late-night picnic in her apartment after meeting each other on the curb at JFK airport. Their flirtatious conversation soon turns to politics. Sweet shares a tape of a young woman he met who is in hiding in Kuwait. She secretly composes songs a capella in her closet to avoid being brutalized by her husband. After hearing the tape, Lauren reveals her fury about the mistreatment of women by religious leaders throughout the world.*

LAUREN: *(Softly.)* Those fucking, murdering . . . *(Opens her eyes.)* It shouldn't take airplanes crashing into skyscrapers — it shouldn't take —

We should bomb them off the face of the earth. Every single one of them —

Off the fucking face of the earth. Sometimes there are people who *are* better, who *are* more evolved, and sometimes those people — no matter the perceived hypocrisy or how ugly — those people should enforce their superiority.

For centuries women have been — in that part of the world — we all know it — it's a holocaust — it's been a holocaust — and if it was heroic, if it was America's proudest moment when we freed the Jews from Hitler and the Nazis, then what kind of historic mission would it be to finally free all the women and young girls being murdered and raped by the princes, mullahs, ayatollahs, and all of their kind?! Why aren't our armies marching into Mecca to save them? Because they're not worth it. Because no one's saying they're worth it. In comparison to the sacrifice. The boys lost. Our economy. A president, a pope could save them all. But fundamentalists are all the same. They like power and the religion that gives it to them. And that's more important than the beautiful girl on your tape and anyone like her. Who does that sound like? Does that sound like a Republican?

BLACK FOREST

Anthony Giardina

More information on this author may be found on the "Meet the Authors" web page at www.smithandkraus.com.

Dramatic
Heidi, fifties to sixties

> *Heidi is the wife of a professor at a college for women. She is incensed about the politically correct requirement that black literature be included prominently in the curriculum because she doesn't think it measures up.*

HEIDI: *(Plowing ahead.)* Oh. Look: is it really necessary to have an entire course devoted to black writing? None of it is that *good*. Am I saying something shocking? I've tried to read those writers, and well — Toni Morrison with her ghosts, and the other one — the lesbian letter writer —

I could name you a dozen better novels published in any year that will sink like stones while students are force-fed this second-rate work. It all goes back to what I said before. We are afraid to say what's true. Somewhere along the line, we stopped being a ruling elite, became terribly self-conscious. Vietnam wounded us, Nixon twisted the knife, and then the culture of money came along and buried us. Who's running this country now, does anyone know? Is it one of those wormy little men whose faces I'm forced to look at just because he affected a great merger or cornered the market on microchips? All I know is it's not us anymore. Not us with our standards and our decency —

CARTOON
Steve Yockey

Seriocomic
Esther, preteen

> Cartoon *is a surreal farce that takes place in a cartoon universe ruled* *by Esther, a bratty little girl who uses a yellow hammer to control her* *unruly toys. Here, she expresses her rather totalitarian political philoso-* *phy as she whacks her toys. (Note: In the original play,* << >> *indicate* *portions of Esther's dialogue amplified through a microphone.)*

ESTHER: What are you doing? Why are you shooting people? <<We need as many people as we can get to look for my hammer.>> Did you hear me? Get back to looking! <<Get moving!>> . . .

And now an educational outreach, a minor distraction, a brief his-tory of the political landscape. . . .

Many years ago, we were a disorganized band of towns. Very tribal, very raw. This loose association of communities was unified by Bolinger the Duck. Bolinger was killed by a foreign power and leadership fell to the Untilololo. But no one could understand anything he said; therefore, he was quickly killed and a rapid succession of leaders followed: Chihuli DeMan, Smirky, Fini Fini, but order was restored by the local chapter 273 of the society of the machete-wielding acrobats. Good people. They were fairly stable and everyone was pretty happy with the government; unfortunately, a power-mad dictator assassinated all of the members of chapter 273. The most controlling, nightmarish, and destructive force that we've ever seen: <<Cynthia.>>
(She pauses for dramatic effect.)

Cynthia ruled with an iron fist for a long time, and public execu-tions were a pretty common Sunday outing. But that's no way to live, and several factions tried to eliminate Cynthia. However, they were all defeated and subjected to the worst punishments imaginable. It's only recently she was overthrown, in a military insurgency . . . by me. . . .

So people disagree about how exactly a government should work. That gave us Bolinger the Duck, Untilololo, Chihuli DeMan, Smirky,

Fini Fini, local chapter 273 of the machete-wielding acrobats, Cynthia, and me.

Because really, people are fickle.

I should say, I think the idea of violence, the fear of it, is a much better motivator than actual violence. That is, in my opinion, where a lot of folks get tripped up. Like Cynthia. Don't get me wrong; I'm totally in favor of hurting people when you need to. <<Just so now you know.>>

THE COLUMBINE PROJECT
Paul Storiale

Dramatic
Mrs. Harris, thirty-five to forty

Mrs. Harris's son was one of the perpetrators of the Columbine High School massacre. She is speaking to the audience as she folds the clothing her son was wearing when he was killed. Her mood is angry, yet calm.

MRS. HARRIS: I have no answers for what my son has done. I am outraged. Embarrassed. I have sorrow. The lawsuits filed against my husband and I speak for themselves. We must pay for the sins, religious, moral, and otherwise, with which my son has commanded unto this world. I extend my personal apologies to the communities in and around Littleton, Colorado, to the nation, and to the world, but no one listens.
(She holds back, a moment.)
As a mother, I have done all I could with the powers existent within me. With the advice of our family doctor, Eric was given a prescription to a drug called Luvox. I trusted this doctor. And, I trusted my son. A mother's intuition. I should have known. BUT I DID NOT KNOW. If I had known what my son had planned, this would never have happened. Eric has played video games since he was a young child. It's what kids do. It was not ignored or avoided. I understood the video games and music Eric purchased were not civilized, but *(She thinks a moment.)* I suppose, I failed. I try not to blame myself, but I failed. Although my son was loved and attended to from the beginning of his life. My husband and I loved our son and gave him as much attention as any parent. We share their hate for our son. It is unforgivable but not foreseeable. We share the sobbing questions, and we share in the grief, but let it be known that we are victims too. The witch hunt against us is . . . Well, it's not fair even so. Their need to punish someone, somehow for this hideous attack is absolutely painstaking. The multimillion dollar lawsuit that the Shoels family brought against us not only hurts but it angers me. Dylan and Eric are dead. They murdered these thirteen people and included themselves. We receive no empathy. We are badgered by blame for something no parent should ever endure yet. I ask myself every day

if there is anything I would change and my answer is no. I was tricked by my own flesh and blood like all of you. And I ask please, don't attempt to pledge me guilty.

The guilty are dead, and I was tricked too.

THE COLUMBINE PROJECT
Paul Storiale

Dramatic
Mrs. Shoels, thirty-five to forty

Mrs. Shoels's son, a black youth, was killed at Columbine High School.

MRS. SHOELS: My son died at Columbine High School. He was called a nigger repeatedly before those boys shot him. It's a word I taught my son means absolutely nothing. A word people use to bring you down. Make you feel bad, so you don't get higher than them. He heard that word over and over and over again in that library in front of all those other scared kids. My son was huddled under that table, tears in his eyes. Since that day, my husband can't sleep in the same bed twice. We're horrified by the phone calls we get, the people driving by our house screaming names I've never heard before. My son was my love. Precious, beautiful, innocent love of his mama's life. I can't help but hate. I start with those boys and I move on to that teacher in the library who could have saved my son and those other kids. Gabbin' on the telephone to the 911 operator for five excruciating minutes, hearing the gunshots get closer and doing nothing but talking to that operator. She could have gotten up and had all the kids help to move tables and desks and equipment against that door, but for five minutes, she did nothing but sit behind that desk, and when they entered? She crawled into a cabinet so she didn't die because she has children of her own. She ain't no hero, she's a goddamn coward! There, I said it. Someone had to. Those kids in that school were the only heroes. That teacher, Mr. Sanders. He was a hero, but that teacher in the library was nothing but a scared mouse hiding in her little hole. The sheriff's office doesn't like me asking questions. Tough shit!

How can you go around making pipe bombs and killing people and not think I wasn't gonna ask questions?

DEAD MAN'S CELL PHONE
Sarah Ruhl

Seriocomic
Jean, forty

*While sitting in a café, Jean picked up and answered an incessantly
ringing cell phone belonging to a man who turned out to be dead. Here,
she talks about the consequences of this action.*

JEAN: You know what's funny? I never had a cell phone. I didn't want to always *be there*, you know. Like if your phone is on you're supposed to be
there. Sometimes I like to disappear. But it's like — when everyone has
their cell phone on, no one is there. It's like we're all disappearing the
more we're there. Last week there was this woman in line at the phar-
macy, and she was like "Shit, shit!" on her cell phone and she kept saying "Shit, fuck, you're shitting me, you're fucking shitting me, no
fucking way, bitch, if you're shitting me I'll fucking kill you," you know,
that kind of thing, and there were all these old people in line, and it was
like she didn't care if she told her whole life, the worst part of her life, in
front of the people in line. It was like — people who are in line at phar-
macies must be strangers. By definition. And I thought that was sad. But
when Gordon's phone rang and rang after he died, I thought his phone
was beautiful, like it was the only thing keeping him alive, like as long
as people called him he would be alive. That sounds — a little — I know
— but all those molecules, in the air, trying to talk to Gordon — and
Gordon — he's in the air too — so maybe they all would meet up there,
whizzing around — those bits of air — and voices.

DON'T TALK TO THE ACTORS

Tom Dudzick

More information on this author may be found on the "Meet the Authors" web page at www.smithandkraus.com.

Comic
Beatrice, sixties

> *Beatrice Pomeroy, a bawdy, blowsy nightclub entertainer, has been cast, or miscast, in a new Broadway play about a sweet, gentle middle American family. In this, her first scene, day one's rehearsal is already underway. The cast has never met their costar, and now here she is — late!*

BEA: OK, here they are, I found 'em, babe, thanks a lot!

Whew! Didn't think I'd ever find it. Will somebody tell me what the hell happened to Broadway?! It's goddamn Disney World out there! Nothin' but tourists! And they're useless! Ask 'em directions, they don't know their ass from their elbow! Who y'gonna ask? Can't find a cop, can't find a hooker. And willya tell me where's all the hookers?! There's fourteen-year-old girls dressed like hookers, but those are the tourists! It's all mixed up! Hi everybody, how are ya', sorry I'm late. Sit, sit. It's this Alexander Graham Bell Hotel, that's the problem. The Eli Whitney, some inventor hotel, who knows! They've invented a new kind of rudeness, I'll tell ya' that. It's on account of them putzes I'm late. See, I checked in last night, walked into my room, made a beeline for the can. I'd been holdin' it since La Guardia. And sittin' on the sink is this little basket of toiletries. Cutest damn thing I ever saw. Eentsie-weentsie bottles, soaps and doo-dads, in this tiny wicker basket with a gingham ribbon. Oh, I couldn't get over it. You don't find that kinda thing at Motel Six, I can tell ya' that. Well, I thought this would make a helluva little gift for everybody here at the first rehearsal. So I called the front desk this morning and asked if they could come up with five more. Big outfit like that, what's it to 'em? "I'm sorry, madam, but if we did that for everyone, we would soon be out of business." Well, you can kiss my ask-me-no-questions, fella!

(Reaches into bag.)

But Pomeroy came through, gang. When in doubt, go to the people. The American way. I started knockin' on doors. And people can be so nice, y'know?

(Pulls a toiletry basket from bag.)

See that? Isn't that adorable? Did a lot of free PR for the show, too. The twenty-first floor knows we're here, I'll tell ya' that! Here, that's for you.

(Hands basket to Mike.)

You the playwright? Here y'go, Shakespeare. There's some bubble bath in there. Now, here's what you wanna do. Tonight, you take a nice soothing soak in the tub with those bubbles, see. Then tomorrow, when you wake up all relaxed, maybe you can come up with a couple of new jokes for Act Two. I'll show you where they go.

DUSTY AND THE BIG BAD WORLD

Cusi Cram

More information on this author may be found on the "Meet the Authors" web page at www.smithandkraus.com.

Comic
Lizzie, eleven

> *Lizzie Goldberg-Jones, a precocious yet charming girl, is speaking to a video camera. The monologue is her entry in a video contest for a very popular kid's television show called* Dusty, *which her little brother Petey is obsessed with. Lizzie and Petey are the children of a male homosexual couple. This is the first time we see Lizzie in the play.*

(Lights up on Lizzie. She speaks to a video camera.)

LIZZIE: For the record: my favorite show is *Sponge Bob*. Sorry, it is. Do you guys watch that show? You should. Sponge Bob, he's like a sponge. He's supposed to be an underwater sponge, but he looks like a dish-washing sponge, and he lives in a pineapple with his pet snail, Gary, and works as a fry cook at the Krusty Krab and has a really annoying neighbor, Squidward Tentacles who's like always taking bubble baths. *(Lizzie laughs, she snorts a little.)* That show rocks. Like sometimes it makes me laugh so hard I snort. Seriously. My dads like to watch the *Gilmore Girls* with us — they're really into the mother, Lorelei. I think she drinks way too much coffee and talks too fast. If my dads talked that much, I'd put myself up for adoption. Honestly. I only watch it with them because we get to watch five hours of TV a week and because they watch the *Gilmore Girls* with me, it doesn't count because it's "family time." I love TV. My dads say too much TV makes you as dense as a Republican. They do. I used to watch *Dusty* when I was little and it was OK. For the record: I don't watch it now and I only said I would [because my brother is] obsessed with Dusty. He has Dusty sheets and PJs and can't go to sleep unless his two Dusty dust balls are tucked under each of his arms. I guess the whole idea of Dusty is kinda neat. I kinda like that he's a dust ball and he's made up of everything and everyone. And it's cool when he pulls some of himself off and then decides to go wherever that particle is from. But [he] travels in a magical dustpan, which is a little lame, a dustpan? And his friend Spuds is lactose intolerant and that's ALL HE EVER TALKS ABOUT but whatever, the show is cool. I mean, if you're six. Petey is six. So, when I heard the show had this competition, I thought, OK, why not? So. Dusty wants to know why he should come and visit us? Why we're special? I guess, first of all because Petey would love it more than anything in the world if you filmed us and then turned us into animated characters. It'd be like *Sponge Bob* — but not as cool. I also thought maybe if the kids at school saw Petey on *Dusty*, saw my whole family animated — then maybe they would stop teasing Petey. It's not like he complains. But stuff bugs him. It bugs me too. People say the dumbest stuff, like it's really weird you have two dads and the Bible says this and that about gay people. And mostly I don't care about the Bible or what other people say because we are agnostic. Buddhists, anyway. But I thought if we were on TV then maybe people would stop saying stupid stuff. Because TV matters. It matters to everyone.

DUSTY AND THE BIG BAD WORLD
Cusi Cram

Seriocomic
Karen, late twenties to early thirties

Karen is someone very much on edge. She is speaking to Nathan Fried-man, the head writer of a popular television show for children called Dusty, *which is produced by PBS. Karen has called Nathan down to Washington, D.C., to leak some information to him. Her boss, who works in the White House, has plans to withdraw funding for* Dusty. *Nathan is a little drunk, and the meeting is not going very well. Here, Karen loses her patience with him and lets it rip. She has been sitting on a lot a secrets, and her irritation at Nathan somehow unlocks a flood of information.*

KAREN: You . . . know what a job can mean . . . People assume a lot. They assume a lot about you because maybe you have hip shoes and a hand-knitted hat and you seem like you have half a brain . . . they assume that you can just make a living . . . that you can have your own life and pay your bills and THAT is a big assumption. These shoes are four years old . . . catch my drift?

Let's just say hypothetically . . . you are a college-educated white woman, working toward a master's degree in something arty — something arty but with some sort of practical application in the workplace. Let's say — hypothetically that you are a part-time graphic design student and you work part-time in a restaurant and your life is on course, you have goals, desires, and just a little bit of talent, which is all anyone really needs to succeed in this great land of ours.

All is well, you are well, and then BOOM you hit a rough patch emotionally. Let's say you find your boyfriend sleeping with your younger, barely legal HOT sister and let's say you kinda fall apart.

You stop paying bills, you stop going to classes, you make it to your part-time job because you need cash, you don't have a rich family, or brother, or grandma in the wings, in fact, your whole family is financially irresponsible and barely scraping by in parts of the country you have no desire to ever live in, like central Florida, for example.

One day, you awaken at ten a.m. and let's say you take your morning Tylenol PM. You have your two glasses of cheap morning Chardonnay with some cold pizza and you realize that you don't have enough white wine or Tylenol PM to get through the day, and it will be a long day as your job at an upscale eatery in Georgetown doesn't begin 'til five p.m. You get in the car to drive to the strip mall where, as luck would have it, there is a CVS AND a package store that sells your particular brand of New York state chardonnay.

Here's the HITCH in your plan. The STITCH in your side. The foil to your foggy state of mind — Somehow as you are driving in your car, listening to, let's say, some trance music you love, DESPITE the fact that your boneheaded ex gave it you — you run through a red light and then in an INSTANT you wake up. You wake up BIG TIME.

The EDGE is in your face. You are at one with the edge. You might even say as the paramedics scrape you and the other people in the four cars that have spun out of control, simply because you were listening to a cool beat and thinking about your morning high, you have BECOME the edge.

And things, let's say things get more complicated, the really complicated thing is that you have not paid your car insurance in two months, and it has been canceled on that very day, that very exact day, hypothetically that is.

Suddenly, your life is not your own anymore, your life belongs to six people who have various internal and skeletal injuries and want to sue your ass off. Let's say and all this is very hypothetical of course, things get even more complicated when you are given a blood alcohol test and your levels are through the roof, because in fact you have been drunk for three months. You barely sleep, despite the Tylenol PM. What you do is drink.

Somehow, through a stream of events which involve rehab and going on welfare and avoiding prison time by taking a vaguely Christian life skills program at a local community center, you find yourself offered a job at the White House. Let's say you are offered this job because the woman who runs the vaguely Christian life skills program has a very, very dear friend who works for the president and that very same woman with the important job believes in giving people second chances because

. . . though it is never stated boldly and clearly in capital letters she had SOME DARKNESS IN HER PAST.

In fact, because you are white and college educated and not addicted to crack she decides to give you a pretty important job with lots of responsibility at least for someone like you — the new "fallen" you.

And because, let's say, you have been truly humbled by life and have done a lot of twelve-stepping, you are filled with a deep gratitude to your new strange Christian boss and have begun to believe that your life may some day be your own again, even though it is not for one second the life you imagined yourself having but it's a lot better than the other lives you have lived since that fateful moment at the intersection — that moment when you became the edge.

Despite your dreams of fame, fulfillment, and having a HOT husband and a HOT career, you have become someone who is simply grateful for a JOB, hypothetically speaking that is.

EMILIE'S VOLTAIRE
Arthur Giron

Dramatic
Emilie, twenties

> *Emilie de Chatelet, the most beautiful woman in France, has a passion*
> *for learning. She has helped the great philosopher Voltaire escape from*
> *Paris and brought him to her chateau, where she hopes to become a sci-*
> *entist under his tutelage, but she is angry with him and here tells him off.*

EMILIE: Your insatiable desire is not flattering to me. In fact, I am insulted by
it. Return to Paris! I will see to it that you get a fresh horse. I don't care
if you face imprisonment, torture even, for saying the queen cheats at
cards. For writing treasonous books critical of all things French! I don't
care if your nose is cut off! I withdraw my protection. A notorious sexual satyr under my roof! No! Don't stay with me. We have no future. A
horse for Monsieur Vulgár! Stop your moaning! Stop it! Love sick, are
you? You are disturbing my household! I humiliated myself going to
your apartment in Paris because I couldn't wait to engage your sparkling
imagination. Mercy?! You haven't a drop of it. Don't you realize that un-
like you, I received no formal schooling. The only way I can learn is by
listening for informative gold nuggets from the lips of wise men. THAT
is my passion! I can find such little pleasure in predictable, conventional
intercourse with the esteemed nobility . . . There must be more to life.
More. I WANT MORE!

EMOTION MEMORY

Don Nigro

Dramatic
Lyka, twenty-six

> *Anton Chekhov has been out walking in the cold all night after the dis-*
> *astrous first production of his play,* The Seagull, *very bitter about the*
> *incompetence of the actors, the stupidity of the audience and the critics,*
> *and the humiliating nature of the theater. Lyka, a friend of Chekhov's*
> *family who is deeply in love with him, is the only one who has waited*
> *up for him all night. She's been trying to convince him that it's a won-*
> *derful play, that he mustn't give up on it, and that in a way it's a good*
> *thing that this theatrical disaster has gotten the usually reserved*
> *Chekhov in touch with some deep feelings. But Chekhov, tired and*
> *upset, has uncharacteristically lashed out at her, suggesting that giving*
> *in to her own feelings has made a mess of her life.*

LYKA: Do you mean that because I tried to kill myself in Berlin I have no right
to feel things? That I shouldn't allow myself to love or feel passion for
someone just because Potapenko deserted me and went back to his stupid wife? Well, I don't care. I loved him and I'm glad I gave myself to
him, and if that meant I had to suffer then I had to suffer, and if it meant
I wanted to die then it meant I wanted to die. But I didn't die and at
least I'm honest about what I feel. It's all right to hate directors and actors and audiences and critics. There's nothing wrong with feeling those
things. When my child died, I wanted to die with her, and there was
nothing wrong with feeling that, either. Don't tell me it was wrong for
me to feel these things, and feel them deeply. This is what normal people do. The rage you felt tonight is a good thing. What you suffered is a
good thing. Bottling everything up and making some sort of wry joke
about it, that's not a good thing. Your play is not a wry joke. There may
be funny things in it, but your play is a deeply emotional experience, and
some day when it's done right, by people who aren't incompetent, in
front of people who aren't cretins, it will be that for them, too. Do you
think I'm blind? Do you think I can't see that it's about me? *The Seagull*
is about me. I'm Nina. I'm the girl who loves the cynical writer who

abandons her. It's me. You wrote about me. But in the play you've reversed it. The writer loves me, but I betray him. Unless you're the older writer who abandons her. Which one are you? Are you both of them? I think you must be both of them. The people I love always turn out to be somebody else, playing some role I've cast them in. It's all a grotesque play. But your play is much more beautiful. And the girl in the play is me. You took my life and put it in a play. At least do me the courtesy of not looking me in the face and lying to me about it. It's the greatest honor anybody's ever given me in my life. To care enough about me to sit down and put me in that world. To take such pains to try and understand me. To give me those incredible words. I'm very, very grateful. Don't tell me what your intention was. It was an act of love. To me, that play means you love me. In some deep part of your soul, you love me, and you know you love me, and you had to write about me, so you put me in that play. I'm not embarrassed. I'm proud. Even if you'll never be man enough to admit it to yourself, I know it's true. It's an amazing gift you've given me. Don't you try and take that from me. I don't care if nobody else understands it. I understand it. I am that girl. It's me.

EMOTION MEMORY
Don Nigro

Dramatic
Lyka, thirty-four

Lyka has appeared on Chekhov's porch at Yalta one evening in 1904. When she was a very young girl, she was desperately in love with him, but he could not bring himself to commit to her, in part because he was alarmed at her depth of emotion. She's had a very difficult life since then, including an affair with a married man, an illegitimate child who died, and a drinking problem. Once she was proud to have been the model for Nina in Chekhov's play, The Seagull, *but now Chekhov has married somebody else, and she's become bitter about her experience with him. And yet she still loves him deeply.*

LYKA: I used to believe in the miraculous healing powers of art. This was during that long period in which I was desperately in love with you. But then I decided that outside of matter there is no truth. That there is only flesh and blood, and vegetation, rain, dirt, and stone. If you're looking for God, I thought, you must find that elusive and possibly imaginary personage in what you can touch. Oh, God, am I quoting you? Did you write that once somewhere? Do you see what you've done to me? Your words have infected my brain, and now I can't tell where you stop and I begin. But you didn't want me, so I gave myself to Potapenko, and then he left me, and I gave myself to my child, and she died, and then I gave myself to Potapenko again, and he left me for good, and then I went back to art and decided to sing opera or dance or do some damned thing. But I realize now that that was all foolishness, so I've given it up. I've given up love and I've given up flesh and I've given up art and all that's left is to drink until I can sleep. Then maybe I can die and have a conversation with Dostoyevsky. Except I hear he was a horrible person, too. You're all horrible people. All of you. Never trust a writer, you told me. I didn't believe you. But you were right. Don't be sorry. You've already been sorry. It didn't do any good, did it? But don't be sad. It's a beautiful play. I've tried to hate it, but I can't, because it's a very beautiful play, and when we're both dead, it will still be there for somebody to open up like a Christmas present. That was your gift to me. It's a cruel gift. But there you are. One loves. One doesn't love. One loves. And there ought to be love in a play. Otherwise —

(Pause.)

I've forgotten my line. You're the playwright. Tell me what the next line is.

FOR OUR MOTHERS & FATHERS
Crystal Skillman

More information on this author may be found on the "Meet the Authors" web page at www.smithandkraus.com.

Dramatic
Donya, fifteen

> *Donya, a seemingly confident and cool teenage girl who is learning guitar at an all-girl rock camp in Ohio, runs into two other teenage girls, Max and Lil, in the middle of the woods. Max and Lil, who were old friends, are trying to figure out what they're going to play at the show for their parents that night. Tensions grow, especially when Lil reveals she will be going to a different college than Max. When Donya innocently mentions that she loves Max's mom's songs (she was a big singer at one point, now teaching at the rock camp despite a clear alcoholic problem), Max explodes in anger. After her outburst, Donya talks about her relationship with her own mother, breaking the silence.*

DONYA: They used to call me Rabbit because I used to try to run away all the time. Like since I was five. Just get the fuck out of my shit town where everyone looks like me and no one, no one is like me. When we applied here I was like — this is it. Just turned fifteen. Practically half my life if I died at forty like my cancer-ridden dad so I thought this would be it. Pack for two weeks? I packed *everything*. And when I was like zipping up my bag I couldn't stop crying. My mom, saw me like that, and we barely talked, she was so soft or something and would just do what he said and then when he was gone, she wouldn't do anything really. If I was a rabbit, she was a mouse. Small to me. The morning I woke up to get the bus to come here — I saw it there on my empty dresser — this old black-and-white photo — a girl about fifteen in this skimpy outfit in front of some tent — and there's like animals in the background and people juggling pins and it's like clear it's some kind of circus. And I know those eyes. It's my mom. My mom. On the back, in this script — her name and the year. She came in the doorway and told me that's when she started to run away. And I was like why didn't you stay and she smiled this weird smile and I liked that it was soft, quiet, and she said because she met my dad and wanted to have me.

And all that I felt in me made sense. And I knew what it was like to want to stay. Because I do feel like that when I write songs — like a part of me is running away and I want to catch her. If it's good I do.

THE FRAMER
Edward Allan Baker

More information on this author may be found on the "Meet the Authors" web page at www.smithandkraus.com.

Dramatic
Patsy, late thirties

> *Patsy is speaking to her picture-framer husband Ronnie, forty, who is dying from an alcoholic-related disease. He has adamantly and unsuccessfully tried to push her away, but Patsy won't leave him or the frame shop, placing her in a delicate emotional state of being.*

PATSY: It's part of who I am, OK, I go with what I got . . . *(Beat.)* I'm half Irish and half Italian, OK, so sometimes I see myself holding you, stroking your face, kissing your forehead just before you take your last breath, and sometimes I see myself ordering you to be buried alive in a landfill. . . . All day, am I Irish? Am I Italian? Irish? Italian? You have no idea what it's like for me! Some nights I go to bed laughing and wake up crying and other nights I go to bed crying and wake up laughing! I'm split about marriage, about S-E-X, about truth and lying, split about love and bitterness, split about living and . . . oh God, thoughts everyday of "Am I better off dead and would anybody care," to being split about *"Oh God let there be a God"* to *"There is no God* otherwise Princess Diana and Mother Teresa wouldn't have died in the same week," to being split every freakin' day "OH NO I'M MY MOTHER" to "No no, I'm more like my father," to the time you're in the mirror thinking, "Shit, I look just awful," and the next day in the *same* mirror, "Oh hey, I'm pretty damn good-looking and feel S-E-X-Y," but yesterday's feeling puts you down, and you return to being . . . half alive . . . Then I come in here and look at the wall of people who had their better sides captured. And we frame them so they can hang 'em up to remind themselves, and that's a good thing, to be less . . . torn up inside . . . so you can . . . I don't know . . . I . . . I don't know why all that came out . . . or if it makes sense . . . I don't know . . .

THE GINGERBREAD HOUSE
Mark Schultz

More information on this author may be found on the "Meet the Authors" web page at www.smithandkraus.com.

Dramatic
Stacey, early to midthirties

> *Stacey is speaking to Collin, a coworker at the travel agency. Collin, who has a crush on Stacey, wants her to teach him all the secrets of what makes a good travel agent, particularly what makes Stacey so exceptionally good. She tells him, and in the process reveals the secret of how she has allowed herself to do some extraordinarily horrible things.*

STACEY: So the question is. What am I doing here? Right? What am I doing here? Why is this my life? Why does my life look like this? Right? Why? You know. Why? And answering these questions. Is really. Difficult. Sometimes. Like. On your anniversary. For instance. And that's the hard part of the job. Really. And the secret to that. Is. Making up a good excuse. A good lie. That you can believe. Or a nice story. That you can tell. To yourself. And to others. To justify. Why here. Why now. Why you. Why obsolete. And if you can't. Well. You're sort of lost.
(Beat.)
   You have to have a story . . .
   What I do is valuable. I tell myself. I am making people happy. I am helping them to be happy. And sometimes people need convincing: they don't know if they really wanna be happy or not. They don't know if they deserve it. So they wanna be told that they're doing the right thing.
(Beat.)
   So here's the secret. Whatever they want. (And sometimes they don't know what they want. And that's tricky. You have to show them. But.) Whatever they want. You say: Yes.
   Yes. But. Then you say: But. Isn't there more. Can't I give you more. Don't you deserve more . . .
   Collin. It is. The worst. Story. Ever.
(Beat.)
   I sold my kids.

THE GINGERBREAD HOUSE
Mark Schultz

Dramatic
Stacey, early to midthirties

Stacey is speaking to Marco, to whom she and her husband sold her children. She has stolen Marco's children in a desperate bid to force him to get her own children back. Marco wants his kids. He says he's willing to be forgiving if she'll just hand them over. But Stacey isn't buying it. She wants him to suffer.

STACEY: I don't want your friendship. Marco. I don't care. About your fucking friendship. About your bridges and your water and your metaphors. Because when your friendship. When your *fucking* friendship. Would have meant something. I came to you. For help. For help. And you refused. You put me out. So you can take your fucking bridge. And your fucking water. And your fucking metaphors. And you can fuck your fucking friendship and say good-bye to your fucking kids. Because until you produce mine. I'm keeping yours. And I'm keeping them safe. And you'll never touch them or love them or see them. Ever. Again.

OK. This is as clear as I can make it. Right? OK? I want. My children. My two children. Back. If I get. My two children. Back. I will give you. Your three children. Back. OK? If I do not. Get. My children. Back. Right? You will not get. Your children. Back. Right? OK? Clear? And I am willing. I am willing. To just say. I am willing. To suffer. Whatever consequences. That entails. It could not be. Any worse. Than what I am going through. Than what I am feeling. Now. So. Know please. That I am so. Fucking. Serious.

IN THE DAYLIGHT
Tony Glazer

More information on this author may be found on the "Meet the Authors" web page at www.smithandkraus.com.

Comic
Charlotte Fontaine, twenty-six

> *Charlotte is a southern girl with a mysterious past. Here, she explains to the Feingold family — Martin, Jessie, and Elizabeth — why she has traveled to New Jersey. It is only later that we find out the actual reason for her visit and her true identity.*

CHARLOTTE: Unfortunately, I've come to in New Jersey to confront my sister Scarlet about some recent credit-card purchases she made without my knowledge. You see, she stole my identity last month and racked up about three thousand dollars worth of colored rocks on my credit card on account of her psychic, Maggie, told her that she was a stone in a past life. It's actually not that hard to believe if you've ever tried to have a conversation with her. What's that? Oh sure, you can come back as all sorts of things. Trees, grapes, most garden equipment, and hair product — a good friend of the family, Emily, is convinced that her little baby, Shawna, who was delivered stillborn just last spring, has come back to life as a George Foreman Grill. Sadly, the grill was ours. She borrowed it and now . . . well, kinda hard to interfere with family, if you see my point. Anyhow, Maggie told Scarlet that the reason why she was feeling so lonely was not because she hadn't had a real date since Bill Clinton was impeached but because she needed to be surrounded by more objects that she could relate to on a "past life" level. So she bought three thousands dollars worth of rocks. Prada handbags, too. Although I don't know where those fit in, metaphysically speaking. My first instinct was to turn it over to the police and let them sort her out. But she's family and turning her out to the cops would have kicked up more dust with my mom, and then my dad would have had a reason to come out of witness protection to put his two cents in — it would have been even more of a mess than it needed to be. I thought about the lessons of family provided in Martin's book and had to admit that since buying those stones,

Scarlet has been doing better — she met Jorge at the Olive Garden where he oversees "dish management," and she's, overall, developed a real positive outlook on life. So, instead of finger-flicking that row of dominoes like I wanted, like my gut told me I should, I just counted back from ten and let a "cooler being" prevail, decided to come on out to the Garden State and handle it like a sister instead of a plaintiff. She is my sister and family is sacred. All you really have is family in the end. When that's gone, what have you got?

IN THE DAYLIGHT
Tony Glazer

Dramatic
Jessie Feingold, twenty-five

> *Jessie is the younger sibling in the Feingold family. Here, she reveals to Martin, her brother, the real reason behind his being summoned home. We learn firsthand that she is not the person we thought she was and see her cold, murderous side for the first time.*

JESSIE: Do you really want to know about that night, Martin? Do you really want all the details? You can't even go upstairs to the bedroom where it happened. How are you going to be able to absorb how I cut that man up? That's right. Mom fell apart. You ran away. I was the only one left. You thought *she* did everything? That's just what we told you. You already hated her for sleeping with another man. If you hated me too, we'd never get you back here, and getting you back here was key. Everything we did was specifically crafted for maximum manipulation. All avenues explored in order to get you back and soften you up once here. Right down to Mom's "oh so mortal" phone call and my "oh so serious" health update. You want to talk about that night? Good. Let's talk about it. Our father was going to kill us all and then kill himself, but he dropped dead before he could do it. Yet while this family suddenly had a second chance, there was still a man shot to death in the bedroom. No matter what story we came up with, we would have never survived the scandal. Dad's legacy, this family's legacy, was in jeopardy. Someone had to do something, so I did it. It was unpopular, it was ugly, but it had to happen. So tell me, Martin. Now that you have your courage up, what else would you like to know about that night? Do you want to know what tools I used? Which ones were great for flesh? Which ones for hacking through bone? Do you want to hear all the trial and error with cutting tools? Why a chain saw, despite popular movie wisdom, is the worst thing to use. Would you like to know how messy it gets with a chain saw? No? How about which corrosive solvents Dad had downstairs that eat flesh and organs without cutting or burning? Products you can buy at any hardware store. How about the bones, Martin? Would you like to hear how, with a hammer, I broke up the bones into little bitty bite-size pieces before systematically burning them all to ashes in Dad's incinerator? Do you want me to itemize the carnage of that night, because I will if it will make you face your own complicity in it. It's truth time, Martin. None of us can move forward until you decide once and for all where you stand. You're going to have to admit to me, admit to us, that you're a part of this family, because without family everything else is a lie. What's it going to be, big brother? Yes or no. In or out.

IN THE NEXT ROOM OR THE VIBRATOR PLAY

Sarah Ruhl

Dramatic
Mrs. Givings, twenties

Mrs. Givings has recently given birth. Here, she is talking to a woman who her husband has hired to be her wet nurse, as Mrs. Givings can't produce enough milk to feed her baby.

MRS. GIVINGS: Of course. Do you want more children, Elizabeth? That is a tactless question, you don't need to answer, forgive me, sometimes I say whatever is in my head. I want more children and my husband desperately wants more children but I am afraid of another birth, aren't you? When I gave birth I remember so clearly, the moment her head was coming out of my body, I thought: Why would any rational creature do this twice, knowing what I know now? And then she came out and clambered right onto my breast and tried to eat me, she was so hungry, so hungry it terrified me — her hunger. And I thought: is that the first emotion? Hunger? And not hunger for food but wanting to eat other people? Specifically one's mother? And then I thought — isn't it strange, isn't it strange about Jesus? That is to say about Jesus being a man? For it is women who are eaten — who turn their bodies into food — I gave up my blood — there was so much blood — and I gave up my body — but I couldn't feed her, could not turn my body into food, and she was so hungry. I suppose that makes me an inferior kind of woman and a very inferior kind of Jesus.

A LEGACY FOR THE MAD
Don Nigro

Dramatic
Senta, late twenties

In this very strange play set in what would appear to be the present, a man and a woman, Rupert and Senta, sit together in the moonlight and seem to be telling the story of their romance. It's a very odd story indeed, but the gist of it is that Senta works in a music store and is very mysterious. Rupert and Senta like to break into a zoo at night, where Senta drives Rupert mad with lust, giving herself to him while a sloth watches, after which she disappears for long periods of time. He's just discovered that she was married. Here, she relates to him the sad tale of her husband's unfortunate demise.

SENTA: It was late one night. He was coming home in a wagon full of sheep, up the steepest part of the hill, in the cold. The path was icy. The horse was startled by an owl. The wagon turned over, the sheep spilled out, and he struck his head on a stone. He was killed instantly. Then came the reading of the will. There was a bowl of lemons on the table. A clock was ticking. It took me a moment to fully take in what I was hearing. He had left us nothing. He left everything to the state asylum for the insane. Every penny. Nothing for me. Nothing for his children. He left every penny to the insane. I asked myself, why would he do this? Who did he know that was mad? Nobody in his family was mad. They were stupid, but they weren't mad. Yet he left everything to the state mental hospital. It was the only crazy thing he ever did in his life, except for marrying me. We were left with no money. No visible means of support. I was forced into a life of selling grand pianos to marching bands. But that wasn't the worst part. The worst part was trying to understand why. What was he thinking? You live with somebody. You believe you know them. You don't know anything. They might as well be invaders from Uranus. Why the mad? Why leave everything to the mad? I searched through his papers, his correspondence. Nothing. No clues. Did he fear he was going mad? Did he hide it from us, all those years, those of us who believed that we knew him, believed he loved us? What was going on in his head? I thought and thought and thought about it. But the truth is, you don't know anybody. And the people you think you know the best are the biggest strangers of all because you have the most profound illusions about them and the deepest need to perpetuate those illusions at any cost. You make up stories in your head about who people are, why they do things. But you never really know. Most of the pieces are missing from the puzzle. All you're left with, in the end, are a box of disconnected fragments, a room full of old saxophones.

LOST GENERATION
Don Nigro

Seriocomic
Zelda, thirty

> *It's 1931, and Zelda Fitzgerald, a beautiful and brilliant southern belle, has been placed in a mental institution by her husband, Scott, who has found it almost impossible to write while dealing with her outrageous and sometimes self-destructive behavior. Zelda's mind is like a carnival ride, with words and images tumbling out in all directions. In fact, she is in some ways a more naturally gifted artist than either Scott or their friend Ernest Hemingway, whom she despises. Here, we see her struggling to make sense of her experience and gradually coming to the realization that she herself can create, too, and on her own terms.*

ZELDA: Is something burning? I keep thinking something's burning. And why are there horse flies on my wedding cake? This place is full of Japanese lanterns, wiener dogs, and owls, and it's burning. I always feel so sorry for the furniture. Being a woman, I understand its position. We make each other into sacred objects. This is madness. But I do wish somebody would kiss me again under the pecan trees. Then I'll make a patchwork quilt they can bury him in. You've got to shrink to get into the garden. But if you get too small, you just go out like a candle. Ernest told Scott a man should only look at his penis in the mirror. But everything looks different in the mirror. It's like Alice Through the Looking Glass, only it's your penis. I wonder if Lewis Carroll's penis looked bigger in the mirror? I wish Alice was here so we could ask her. He must have shown her his penis at one time or another. That's what men do when they want you to love them. They show you their penis. What an honor. I named his testicles Tweedle Dum and Tweedle Dee. Tweedle Dum hangs a bit lower, due to an unfortunate mishap involving a revolving door at a delicatessen on 42nd Street. I should stop talking so much about penises. I give myself good advice, I just don't follow it. But in my defense, consider the source. I feel like I'm being devoured by eucalyptus trees. I try to remember not to eat the flowers. The most beautiful flowers are poison. We should go to the circus, get drunk with Spanish clowns, and drive over fireplugs with gypsies in clown cars. I was named for a gypsy queen. I spent my youth on roller skates. I wasn't afraid of anything and I had no morals whatsoever. I was absolutely free. My sisters and I would take baths on the back porch. Boys would gape over the fence. Mother said let them. Be proud of your bodies. The wind strips the trees. Cobbles after rain. Shut the windows against the rain. You don't understand what's happening until it's too late, and then somebody's sticking brightly colored pins in your eyes. I've written you, you said, so you belong to me now. He opened me like an oyster.

Falling headfirst down the chasm
melodies of ghastly spasm.
I've been through the looking glass.
If you don't like it, kiss my ass.

That's actually not bad. I could be a better poet than Wallace Stevens, and punch Ernest in the nose on the quarter hour, like a cuckoo clock. I used to think I was nothing without Scott. Now it turns out I'm nothing with him. I tried screaming in his ear, but he was busy drinking whiskeys at the Susquehanna in Hackensack, trying to start a cock fight. As a woman, I'm always the only adult in the room. Of course, the room is empty. But at least it's mine. Do I hear carousel horses? Somebody save me the waltz. That's a good title. I should write a book.

LOVE DRUNK
Romulus Linney
More information on this author may be found on the "Meet the Authors" web page at www.smithandkraus.com.

Dramatic
Karen, twenties

Karen is a hitchhiker. She has met a much older man named Wilbur in a diner, and he has brought her up the mountain to his house. Here, she describes meeting a local woman, who took her to a church.

KAREN: I got here with a man I met up north. We stopped at that creek to drink and gig frogs with little spears, like we bought at a store. But it was dry. He drank too much. I drank too much. We fell out. He didn't want to go, but I screamed at him and he did. In the morning, a woman was standing there looking at me. "You're lucky you're alive," she said. "Come on with me." She took me to a cabin. Her name was Jean Buel. She heated water on a woodstove. She fed me cornbread and coffee. You don't believe me . . .

There were splinters on the floor around years-old linoleum. The air smelled like smoked wood. I washed with some kind of soap that stung . . .

She was alone. No husband, no children, at least that I could see, living on God knows what. . . .

Why did she take me in? It was Sunday. She wanted me to go to church with her, that's why. What could I say? We went to her church. It was just another cabin, with a sign on it. Amalgamation Saints of God. I never saw such people. They were bad off. Their Walmart, Dollar clothes in rags, their eyes staring out of their heads at nothing. The preacher didn't say much at first. There wasn't any order of worship. They just sang hymns, at the top of their voices, and testified, dripping guilt and self-pity. I thought next, they'll handle snakes . . .

This preacher looked like, I don't know, the Scarecrow in the Wizard of Oz. He talked about Jesus coming again sooner than you think. About burning in eternal fire forever. Then, of all things, he talked about a dry-goods store where they stock little rubber balls. He held two of them up, one in each hand, saying I just love to squeeze these here little rubber balls. I don't know why, but they help me to pray and they help me to love. And them what loves a lot, squeeze, squeeze, gets forgived a lot, squeeze, squeeze. I almost laughed out loud. Jean Buel wasn't laughing. She was crying, leaning on me, tears streaming down her fat face. There I was, in church again with a sanctimonious mother. The saints were nodding and shaking their heads, yelling out ugly hymns. Ridiculous, stupid, ignorant bottom-of-the barrel hillbillies, loving a lot, getting forgiven a lot, robbing each other, screwing each other, and their children! Just like everybody else! And then, oh then, the worst. Rock bottom! The preacher shuts his eyes. Everybody shut their eyes. He raised one arm. They raised one arm. He shivered and shuddered. He said God is in here right now. They shivered and shuddered. There was a long, utter silence. They put down their arms. Smiles and sighs. Silence and peace. They were out of their awful lives! I was left in mine! Me, loving a lot and never getting forgiven a thing. I got out of there. I caught a ride. I told the guy to stop at a rest stop where truck drivers fuck each other in the woods and let's do it. He wouldn't do it and left me in town. I went to the Green Frog Café, looking for someone else, the first fool I could find.

MAHIDA'S EXTRA KEY TO HEAVEN

Russell Davis

More information on this author may be found on the "Meet the Authors" web page at www.smithandkraus.com.

Dramatic
Edna, forties to fifties

> *Edna is alone in her house when a young Iranian comes to the door. This turns out to be Ramin, who is looking for his sister, Mahida, currently out on a walk with Edna's son, Thomas. While Edna and Ramin wait for Mahida's return, they find that they have little in common, and the discomfort and wariness between them grows.*

EDNA: Hm. I do believe you sound rather resentful. . . .

Rather excessive, I would say, in your criticisms. Just because we have a few aberrations here in our country, some misconceptions, as you say, that doesn't mean there's no God, no. Every place on earth, every land, has its problems with its misconceivers. Misguided politicians, or leaders, you know that yourself. You have those sheikhs over there with seventy-five offspring. Who else is spreading themselves like that all across the world? It's a matter of degree. To what degree is a nation of people misconceivd. And as far as that goes, for all the problems, there is no question, I'm afraid, what's Western is the least, by far, misconceived. On this earth. In comparatison, everything else is positively benighted. This country is the light of the world. What we have here. And if that light is misconstrued, or made murky, by certain reprobates in our land, nevertheless, this nation is still the basis, in fact, upon which the human race is most likely to proceed. Otherwise, it's all dogs and darkness and barbarians out there. It's as simple as that. And if we don't pay attention to that, what's howling out there at our gates, well, then I'm sorry, we're in for it all over again, another one of those huge collapses, an apocalyptic dark age, I say.

NEW JERUSALEM
David Ives

Dramatic
Rebekah, twenties

Baruch Spinoza is on trial for heresy. Here, his half sister lays into him for his heretical behavior and beliefs.

REBEKAH: Half sister. Not sister. And I'd be ashamed to be half cousin, half anything, half nothing to this noisemaker. This icicle. This prig. And if the regulations say he has to go to the community first, then he's violated the regulations and he should be expelled. And while you're at it, get me the money I should have inherited from my father that's going to him. Or do I have to bypass the Jews and go to the city, like him? Oh, he'll tell you what he needs to say — for him. For Baruch Spinoza. The center of the universe. Yes, the business is bad for this cause and that cause, which depends on this other cause. Maybe business is bad because Baruch is running the business. Maybe Baruch is the cause. And now he says that he's in love? I'm not going to say what he's in love with. One of them. A gentile. A shikse, as our eastern cousins would say. I say Baruch Spinoza does not love anything. Not his family, not his people, not his religion. Ask him about his people. Go on. Ask him about the Jews. Oh, yes, he likes to rub shoulders with the Jews — so he can feel superior to the Jews. Baruch Spinoza hates the Jews. The law of Moses? He despises it. The Jews, he'll tell you? A superstitious people born and bred in ignorance. Just ask him. The Jews? They don't know what God is. The Jews? They have the gall to think of themselves as God's chosen people. The Jews, he will tell you, are no different from anybody else. They're no different from Hindus or Chinese or Christians (Indicating Valkenburgh.) like this piece of paper. Ask Mr. Know-It-All about the Jews. But what he answers, we won't understand. We Jews are too ignorant for his wisdom. We're too superstitious, we're too stupid, we pay too much attention to the sacred books given to us by God. You know he's got Jews stabbing him in the street now, calling him a heretic? What are you waiting for? The Messiah to say he's a heretic? He was a snot when he was a child, and he's still a snot. The arrogance behind all that cheerfulness.

The smugness. Ask him. Somebody. Ask what he really thinks about the Jews and you'll see what he is. This loser. This prince. This fox. Ask. Meanwhile, I say this to him.

(She spits at Spinoza.)

I demand justice. I demand excommunication.

NEXT FALL
Geoffrey Nauffts

Dramatic
Arlene, late forties

> *Arlene's son is in a hospital on life support. While she waits with her*
> *husband and her son's friends, she talks about the guilt she feels about*
> *something that happened in the past between her and her son.*

ARLENE: I Just need a little more time to . . . pray. I'm one, too. Does that surprise you? At least I think I am. Who knows anymore. There's so much
sadness in the world, so much pain, you know? How could anyone allow
it? But then I grab hold of this thing. So familiar. Like an old friend. I
read a passage I've read a thousand times before . . . It gives me comfort
somehow. Butch is a whole other story. He really holds onto the damn
thing for dear life. Poor guy. He wasn't always so fanatical. I'm sure that's
my fault, too. Just another victim of Lung Lady's evil ways. *(A beat.)*
That's something I started calling myself after we split. I was a bit of a
loose cannon back then. We both were. Butch and me. At a certain
point, Butch had enough, and started to pull himself together, while I
sank further into it all. I'd disappear for days at a time. Weeks even.
Then six months in jail. For selling pot. Not even selling, really. Oh, it's
a long, stupid story, involving my ex-best friend, a one-armed beautician
from Shreveport, I kid you not, and a couple of kilos of Maui wowee,
but I was just a fool. Mad at the world and no one was gonna tell me
otherwise. Not even this sweet, little kid. When I got out, I was so de-
termined to make it up to him, I scraped together some cash, and
bought him a bicycle. It had the training wheels, the sparkly tassels, the
wicker basket, and everything just like he wanted, and he wouldn't look
at the damn thing. Just sat in his sandbox, ignoring me. I started stomp-
ing my foot and screaming at the little shit. "Now, you listen to me,
young man." Like, all of a sudden, I was gonna be a parent, right? Well,
Luke wasn't having it, and he shouts back, "No, you listen to me, Lung
Lady." Well, we just glared at each other for a minute, like a couple of
mules, then I just fell out laughing. And I thought, you know he's right.
That's what I've become. One of those evil cartoon characters. Cigar

chomping, tits out to here, fire shooting out my metallic bustier. With dark and mysterious powers no one would ever understand. Lung Lady. Of course, that's not what he meant, but somehow it all made sense and the name sorta stuck. Eventually, I worked my way into the sandbox with him. He's sitting there, all angry and defiant, just like his momma, and suddenly I can't speak. Afraid I might break him. Or lose him. He pushes his little toes up against mine, and asks if people can glue their feet together. And I say, "Well, now why would anyone wanna do that?" And he looks up at me with these big eyes and says, "So no one can ever separate us." Well, that just took my breath away. And I realized I had to leave again. Because I wasn't ready. Wasn't sure I ever would be. So, Lung Lady crawled back into her hole for another ten years until she was ready to resurface. Butch met Lynn not long after, so Luke finally had some . . . stability. Of course, who can recognize her now with all the work she's had done, but she's a good mom, I guess. Gave him a little brother who adores him. And me, I've spent years trying to figure out how to make it all up to him.

THE OPTIMIST

Jason Chimonides

More information on this author may be found on the "Meet the Authors" web page at www.smithandkraus.com.

Seriocomic
Nicole, twenties

> *Nicole encounters her ex-boyfriend, Noel, during the weekend of their mutual best friend's funeral. Here, after the service, Nicole confronts her mortality and seeks Noel's help in the process.*

NICOLE: *(A discovery.)* I need for you to be my friend for five minutes. I'm really confused and I just need to be able to say stuff and not have to know what it means! OK?! And you don't either! *(Beat.)* OK?! . . .

And I don't want you to, like, start twisting it and using it to make yourself miserable. *(A beat. She stares at him.)* . . .

I'm seriously asking you. Can you be my friend and help me sort some shit out . . . even though that shit is related to, stems from, and is completely actually because of you? *(A beat.)* . . .

I really need for you to tell me something about us that I don't remember. . . .

Remind me of something I've forgotten. . . .

I don't know why. Because. . . .

Because I'm afraid I'm forgetting my life. *(Beat.)* Or . . . not forgetting exactly . . . I mean, I still remember what my mom looks like and what my pin number is, but my experiences, you know? . . . It's like . . . OK: Wilfredo, right? Wilfredo Capellini, my first boyfriend and . . . this weird little African song he taught me on his thumb piano . . . or my dad back when he was still a pothead and used to play the guitar . . . or getting fired from Epcot in the tenth grade because I called that little girl a "bitch" . . . they all just pool up — these moments, this stuff — they all just pool up and drain away, pool up and drain away, and sometimes it feels like so little remains. So little feeling. It's as if . . . it was me, of course it was, but sometimes it feels like it was someone else's life. Where did it all go? *(Slight beat.)* And it's hitting me — I'm not preparing anymore. For life. It's in session, you know? It's happening. And I know it sounds so stupid, but sometimes I feel like I wasn't even around for it. Like it's empty. *(A beat.)*

OR
Liz Duffy Adams

Comic
Lady Davenant, forties to fifties

Lady Davenant (in historical fact the first female theater manager) has dropped in unexpectedly on Aphra Behn, a poet and ex-spy eager to break into the theater. She speaks without pausing, even when asking a question; not so fast that she can't be understood, but without giving Aphra a chance to speak. She is imperious, high status, keenly interested in Aphra's potential to make her money, and not without a genuine love of the theater.

LADY DAVENANT: Hello darling hello you must be Mrs. Behn, forgive me forgive me horribly ill-mannered I know I know my dear late Lord D used always to tell me but I thought I'd just pop in to say but O of course you must think I'm a madwoman I haven't introduced myself Lady Davenant, Duke's Company you know — I won't unmask, just swooping in on my way to see what king's has up and it won't do to have 'em see me in the house taking notes — well but I've heard all about you, setting up for a poet, love your nerve darling love your *guts*, sign of the new age isn't it, sign of the times, women kicking over the traces and damn the naysayers and why not, darling, why not, look at me, my dear late Lord D passes on and everyone expects me to sell the license but ho, I say, ho ho, why should I not carry on as before after all there's nothing much to it, choose the plays keep the players sober within reason and hollah, the money rolls in; after all Johnny does most of the work, Johnny Downes our prompter, he bullies 'em through their paces with his bell and whistle and what have I do to but count the gate? and I can count I assure you though I wasn't raised for it but who could be married all those years to my dear late Lord D without sharpening her wits, a lovely man but O as practical as a spring hare I assure you a mad *bunny* would have been more rational — you've no view here do you well what does a poet want with a view, inward views no doubt inward views — mind you why should he be practical, a great man, a great trainer of actors, a great man of the theater, you know he was the natural son of the great man himself, O yes, not much of a secret so I don't mind telling you, the natural son of Mister Shakespeare himself so there it is, blood will tell, but genius is rarely sensible so I learned to count for sheer self-protection and I will tell you darling it is the most useful skill I could have mastered and I recommend it to you heartily if you haven't learned it so there it is I'm the queen of Dukes as the joke goes and I need a play; that scatterwit sotted dog Shadwell — I abuse him though I love him — promised me one and sugar-talked me into booking it and all and what does the fool do but get himself clapped by a Holborn drab, he's in the country sweating it out of himself and swears he cannot finish the play so there it is, can't leave the playhouse empty it's a hole in my pocket, rehearsals begin tomorrow, I can give you Lizzie Barry for a lead and you won't find better, say what you will of Nellie Gwynne, Lizzie is a honey and the wits adore her, give her the prologue and you won't be hissed off at the start and that's half-way there, I'll give you the usual third-day's profit and not a penny mislaid, I see to it myself, well? have you a play for me? is that it? nearly finished is it? finish it by morning? cutting it fine darling cutting it fine but there, I'm a soft touch, I'll take a flyer on you only don't be late, mustn't keep actors waiting around without the play they'll start to drink then it's quarrels and misbehaving behind the scenery and asking to go home early — utter utter chaos darling, never leave actors with nothing to do, remember that — get me the thing by let's say nine on the clock and if it's any good at all we'll have an agreement and O what sort of play is it, comi-tragedy, yes? that's good, beginning to go out of style but the people still love a comi-tragedy and if you'll take my advice you'll pad it out with a song or two, give everyone a chance to buy an orange and fondle their neighbor without fear of missing something important, you know the sort of thing (*Goes right into singing without a pause, shockingly loud.*)

HO! THE WORLD GOES ROUND AND ROUND!
HI! AROUND AND ROUND IT GOES!
HA! THE WORLD GOES ROUND AND ROUND!
HEY NINNY! NINNY! NINNY!

Well not that but you see what I mean, and O one other thing I won't have one of those "or" titles, you know what I mean, one of those greedy get-it-all-in titles, "the something something OR what you something," I don't care if the great man did it, they take up half the poster and the typesetter charges by the word, make up your mind and pick one, thank you; now understand me darling this is a rare opportunity, a lucky chance, if you can't deliver me the thing in time I'll be horribly vexed and I don't know when I'll have another chance for you and you know kings don't need you, dukes is your only hope; mind you they clamor me Who is she What sort of education Jumped-up nobody from nowhere and I say well who was Mister Shakespeare hah! and that lays 'em by the heels so remember that darling and don't let 'em fright you; I've seen your poetry, you've got the spark all right, don't let anyone tell you otherwise but it don't do anyone any good if you can't write "the end" and get on with it; there that's what I came for lovely chatting I feel we're friends already must fly don't mind showing me out just write! Write! Write! Write! Write!

PRETTY THEFT

Adam Szymkowicz

More information on this author may be found on the "Meet the Authors" web page at www.smithandkraus.com.

Dramatic.
Allegra, eighteen

> *Allegra is talking to her father who is in the hospital in a coma. Allegra's friend Suzy was going to come to the hospital with her but instead went to the movies with Allegra's boyfriend. Allegra knows this.*

ALLEGRA: And I'm working at this like group home with Suzy Harris. We hang out a lot. You know who she is? I think you'd like her. She's a lot of fun. She was supposed to come here with me today but . . . she couldn't make it. Bobby's good. He works at the garden place in Salem sometimes on the weekends. He wishes he could be here too. He's uh . . . a good boyfriend. I think it'll last for us. One of the great . . . things.

Fuck! It's just as hard to talk to you now that you can't talk back. I can't ever say the right thing to you. You're just so . . . not there, aren't you. You always ignore me. I know even if you can hear me right now, you're not paying attention. You never . . . Why don't I matter to you? What do you want from me?!! Maybe you just want to be left alone. Well, that's what I'll do then. I'm sorry I disturbed your deathbed you selfish fucking bastard! You self-centered, egotistical, pompous, fucking bastard! I don't care what you want! I hope you die! I hope you fucking die real soon! You can fucking rot and be eaten by worms! I hope fucking worms eat you! Worms with big fucking teeth! And rats and flies and vultures! I hope vultures dig you up and take you out of the casket and fly away with you! You fuck!
(Pause.)

I miss you. I've always missed you. I'm sorry. I don't want you to die. I'm sorry. I'm sorry. Oh, Christ, I'm so sorry. Please don't die. You're so small. Please, Daddy.

PRETTY THEFT
Adam Szymkowicz

Dramatic.
Allegra, eighteen

> *Allegra is talking to her mother. Her father has just died, and she's taking off on a cross-country trip with her friend Suzy instead of going to the funeral.*

ALLEGRA: I know you're probably mad at me for leaving before the funeral, but I just can't do it. My whole body itches and it won't stop until I get in a car and can't see this house or this town or this state from the rearview window. This way is better. This way I'll come back from my trip and go straight to school and you won't have to look at me or think about me. You can tell people you have a daughter but you won't have to talk to me on the phone or see me on the couch. I'll be a no-maintenance daughter just like you always wanted. I'm going to go now. I know someday you'll want to talk to me again. Maybe after I graduate and get a job and get married and buy a house and have my own daughter. Then you can talk to her and be her favorite and then we can pretend you were a really great mother. She won't know and I don't have to tell her. But now I'm going to get on the road and push you out of my mind and I probably won't think of you until I get to the Grand Canyon or some other fairly good canyon and maybe I'll cry in front of the mammoth orange hole in the ground or maybe I'll smile because it's so beautiful and I'm free and windswept. But first I'm going to get into Suzy's mom's car and we'll drive till there's just drops left in the tank and as we cross the border into Massachusetts, we'll roll into the first gas station where I'll get some Ding Dongs and some orange soda and I'll bite into the first one sitting on the hood, watching the car slurp up gas. Then I'll get in the driver's seat and put my foot on the accelerator until I can't keep my eyes open anymore. So I pull over and we both close our eyes and sleep until we're awoken at three a.m. by separate but equally terrible nightmares.

PUSSY
Laura Jacqmin

More information on this author may be found on the "Meet the Authors" web page at www.smithandkraus.com.

Dramatic
Margot, twenty

Margot is an American college student studying abroad. She is speaking to Alistair, a very proper British MA student she met in a pub just a few hours earlier. After Alistair is punched in the face by a stranger, they head back to his apartment to tend to his wound. Although Alistair still wants the evening to end romantically, Margot can't get out quickly enough, finding herself more attracted to the puncher than the punchee.

MARGOT: I get all these e-mails from my friends, you know? Also doing study abroad? In Spain and Italy and France? I get these e-mails and they're like, *Met a dark, handsome man. A dangerous man with a dicey past. This man is trouble.* And I believe them, because why wouldn't I? And the sex they have is epic. They need lube where they've never needed lube before. They miss class. They blow off trips to museums because they're so busy fucking in the broken-down, romantic, rust-stained flats of these dangerous men who smoke European cigarettes and have scarred knuckles, and the whites of their eyes are enormous and the pupils are dark pits. They fuck like they've never fucked before, and the fact that they're fucking strangers makes it better because it's crazy. It's crazy to sleep with an unknown person who radiates something . . . worrisome. It is violent and unwholesome and half terrifying. You're fucking someone who might murder you and it's fantastic and amazing and something to blog home about. In France and Italy and Spain. *(Beat.)*

And I came to England. There is tea in England. And a certain breed of cow which is pleasing to the eye when it dots the hillsides. And the bottoms of the pint glasses say they were certified to hold a mathematically perfect pint by the Queen herself. I am not sure I am having the adventure I was meant to have.

RAT WIVES
Don Nigro

Seriocomic
Janet Achurch, thirty-two

We are backstage at the Avenue Theatre in London, late on a blustery night in the autumn of 1896, just before a performance of Ibsen's Little Eyolf. Four actresses are preparing to go on, when Janet Achurch, tall, blond, and voluptuous, with a wayward actor husband, Charles, and a drinking problem, discovers that Mrs. Patrick Campbell has been conspiring with the help of the other two actresses, Florence Farr and Elizabeth Robins, to take Janet's part away from her and move the show to the West End for a much more lucrative run without her. Janet is enraged and bitter and has started drinking again. This is the role of her life. She can't bear to give it up, and she's furious that the others have, in her eyes, betrayed her.

JANET: It's theater that will kill me some day. Charles had the bright idea to take me on a grand theatrical tour of Australia, New Zealand, and Tasmania. All the great Tasmanian theaters. He thought there must be money in it somehow. It turns out they are not particularly big on Shakespeare in Tasmania. I was dreadfully ill, but we had to keep performing to pay our way home. They kept me going with alcohol and morphia until we got back to England, where the doctor informed me that my problem was an addiction to alcohol and morphia. Getting this role was such a great thing for me. And now you've stolen it from me. Stabbed me in the back. Stabbed me in the front. Stabbed me in my big, fat ass. The fact remains that I am doing the best work of my life here, in this wretched, dismal, wonderful clat-farting play, so of course you all feel compelled to conspire with a bunch of damned men to betray me so you can get rich dragging poor old Ibsen off kicking and screaming to the West End. We're doing a great thing here. We're doing Ibsen, difficult, boring, drab, cranky old Ibsen, and we're doing it as well as anybody has ever done it in the history of the world, and the first chance you three stupid whores get to cut my throat and take my part away and ruin it all, you jump at it, so goddamned anxious to make yourselves slaves once again to those greedy West End bastards with money in their pockets and shit between their ears. Aren't you the least bit ashamed of yourselves?

REASONS TO BE PRETTY

Neil LaBute

Seriocomic
Steph, twenties

> *Steph has recently left her boyfriend, Greg, because of a casual remark
> having to do with her looks she heard he made to one of his friends.
> Here, she tells him why they are no longer a couple.*

STEPH: Shut up! Shut your big sideways-grinning mouth, that's what I want
you to do. OK?! *(Beat.)* Keep your damn mouth closed for a minute and
listen to me . . . *(She scrambles into her purse, looking for something.)* . . .
(She digs a bit more and comes up with a piece of paper.) Here. This. This
is what I wanted. Here. *(Opening it.)* I've made this over the last however long . . . I dunno, since I left, and it covers all your shit. All the crap
I'm feeling about you but have held my tongue on . . . I was gonna
e-mail you, but this here is way better. *(Looks around.)* People! Hey you
guys over there, check this out . . . I want you all to hear this, this is
good. . . .

  Sit down, Greg, and listen for once. This might help you with your
next girlfriend. . . .

  (Reading.) "Greg, your hair is thinning — I'm a hairdresser so I
should know. You try and hide it pretty well but I can spot it, at the
crown when you're bending over or as you sit in the kitchen eating and
you ask me to get up and fix you something, then I see it. Two years,
that's what I give it. And in front, too, but that may hold . . ."

  "I don't like your eyes. I never have. I think they're small and pig-
gish and you make it worse by squinting a lot. If you ever wore the sunglasses I bought you for Christmas — they were fucking expensive — it
would help but you don't so your eyes look like shit and you're starting
to get wrinkles there, too. Your nose. Where do I begin with your nose?
It's your mom's so I should be kind, but hey . . . fuck that. Your nostrils
make me sick and I always have to look up into them because we have
the most unimaginative sex that a person could ever come up with . . .
I think you're gay, maybe — seriously, you should check into that because you sure have trouble doing it with me and I'm fine. I know I like

it, even with you, so I'm guessing it's you. Your teeth are OK — just — but I don't like your lips at all. Your mouth is wide and your lips are way too thick to be sexy and I hate kissing you. This is a shame but it's true. I've hated kissing you from almost the first time we did it and that's really depressing. Your tongue is like this little poker and you move it too fast and . . . well, you get the idea. It sucks." *(To him.)* Greg. Are you listening? . . .

Good. *(Reads.)* "I've never thought you had a great body, it's OK, but nothing really special and I hate how you walk around — not just at home but outside during the summer or at the gym; a lot, anyway — like you are super cute or something, like you have all these muscles and a nice stomach or whatever, you don't. You never have, so stop doing that. It's kind of pathetic; I am not the only person who thinks that . . . I'm not gonna be so crass as to say much about your dick because that would put me on your level — being hurtful — but I will say this: You're way too hairy down there and most girls find that disgusting. Your balls, too, it kind of makes me gag when I go there. I guess there's nothing you can really do about that — guys don't wax or anything like we do — but you should be aware of it, anyway. It's gross. Enough said. Your legs are fine, probably one of your best features . . . your feet are the worst, though. They are. Your toes are, they're like, almost like fingers and you bite your own toenails — I know you do, I've seen you — and that goes down as the most disgusting fact I know. The fact that you rip off your toe nails with your teeth . . . and then eat them, or nibble at them, anyway, after you've done it. And sometimes you smell. A little . . . You do because you think that you don't have to shower after work and you'll get in bed and sleep and sweat some more and then use a little deodorant and off you go, like, to work or wherever. And so you stink, kind of, but I've stopped speaking about it to you because you don't listen. You do not fucking listen." *(Waiting.)* I guess that would be it . . .

ROUGH SKETCH

Shawn Nacol

More information on this author may be found on the "Meet the Authors" web page at www.smithandkraus.com.

Seriocomic
Barbara, thirties

> *Barbara is speaking to Dex, a coworker for whom she is developing strong feelings and with whom she's locked together in the offices of the animation studio that employs them both. Dex, a former children's author, has just explained his cheerful apathy and his belief that "something could come along" to inspire him. In this moment, Barbara reveals her ambitions and a plan to save their studio's next big family film by rendering a difficult sequence of their little heroine weeping.*

BARBARA: I have a Masters in product design from Pratt where I discovered my aesthetic was inappropriate for adults. Toys taught me to abandon my scruples. I spent my first six months here sculpting maquettes. Then I got to render clothing and foliage in crowd scenes and the tail movements of a minor character: an amusing scorpion featured in the preview for seven-tenths of a second and mentioned favorably in the trades. I spent eight months learning the Tank's software package so that Spence would review my portfolio again and move me out of Character Modeling to Segments. And now while the trees are frozen and everyone is gone and I have the run of a supercomputer that can animate individual snowflakes in a blizzard, I have an opportunity to personally execute a three second sequence that will change the impact, no, the *import* of this very major three-hundred-million-dollar motion picture enterprise, and if I have to camp in my cubicle and live on crystals, I am going to make this the most sensational, significant, cinematic droplet of liquid in the history of the silver screen. I am (what was your word?) *imagineering* my future. You are a witness. My tear.

ROUGH SKETCH

Shawn Nacol

Seriocomic
Barbara, thirties

> *Barbara is speaking to Dex, a coworker for whom she has developed strong feelings and with whom she's locked together in the offices of the animation studio that employs them both. Dex, a former children's author and recovering alcoholic, has discovered that Barbara has dark plans for their studio's next family feature. Dex has just argued that people have always secretly hoped that inanimate objects are alive around them. In this moment, Barbara examines that belief closely.*

BARBARA: Dex, the world isn't alive. Objects aren't animated. This spoon isn't hearing me or wishing for its drawer. You only go halfway. You want everything to have feelings but simultaneously for yours to be the center of attention. So your pencil is lonely, but not as long as you're holding it. So it's alive, but not as alive as *you*. Which means you're surrounded by inanimate slaves that only come to life when you pay attention to them. That isn't hopeful, that's horrifying. If the whole world has feelings then why should any feelings matter more? You are no more alive or special than the weeds that will grow out of your corpse when you decompose. These animated movies we help to manufacture are popular because they are a pleasant fiction that dissolves under scrutiny. It is that kind of pleasant fiction that keeps people from throwing themselves off bridges or drinking Drano. You're made up of atoms and the atoms made up of particles and those particles are only a minute fraction of a percent of your total mass. You are 99.9999999999999999 percent nothing, Dex. And so is your daughter. So is everything. These animated inventions are a Band-Aid that holds all the nothing together. A film is just a series of cels. There are spaces between them. The story is in the spaces. Your little girl was upset because she sensed a basic truth. The same truth that makes you *thirsty*. The world is cold, meaningless, and constructed of clever nothings. For one second, before she was old enough to know, your daughter saw, Dex.

THE SAVANNAH DISPUTATION
Evan Smith

Dramatic
Mary, fifties to sixties

> *Mary lives with her sister, Margaret, who has recently come to doubt her
> Catholic faith when Melissa, a young door-to-door evangelist, comes to
> call. She decides to set a trap for Melissa by inviting her back — and
> also inviting the priest at her church, who, she is sure, will demolish
> Melissa's arguments about religion. The priest does show Melissa up, but
> he also upsets Mary by informing her that she herself doesn't know some
> of the basic tenets of Catholicism.*

MARY: You mean we went through all of this — Why should I go to hell?!
What have I ever done to deserve going to hell? I never murdered anybody. I never robbed a bank. I go to church. I put money in the collection plate. But everybody thinks I'm going to hell. And not because I'm
Catholic or not Catholic. You all think I'm going to hell because I'm
mean. I'm the meanest woman in the world because I won't tip waitresses who don't refill my tea, and I slam the door on Girl Scouts selling
dry little cookies for seven-fifty, and I fight with the checkout girl when
she scans my groceries at the wrong price. So I'm the Wicked Witch of
the West. Well, I'm not! I try to be nice. I try to be nice to everybody,
but sometimes I simply cannot. There is some chemical in my brain that
says, "Let 'em have it!" And when that happens, there's nothing I can do.
The only thing that ever stopped that was Prozac, but it gave me
headaches, so I stopped taking it. So that's how I know it's a chemical
that makes me act the way I do, and why should I go to hell for some
chemical in my brain? If everything we do is just chemicals, why should
anybody go to hell? If this is all some great big huge *test*, then why isn't
it *fair*? Why is *she (Pointing at Margaret.)* born with a sweet disposition?
Everybody talks about how sweet Margaret is; Margaret is a saint; when
Margaret dies she'll go straight to heaven. *(To Margaret.)* You don't even
know you're being good! *(To the others.)* She doesn't check her receipt
when she leaves the grocery store. They could overcharge her on every
thing she buys, and she'd never know. I check every single price, and if

it's off by one penny, I go back and raise hell. That is the way I am; that is the way the Lord made me. It's not my fault. And you have the nerve to tell me I'm going to hell. I've been going to Blessed Sacrament for forty years, and what have any of y'all ever done for me? At least she *(Pointing to Melissa.)* is doing what she can to save my soul. At least she cares! When I think of what I could have done! When Larry left me — for that Baptist woman — *(She shoots a glance at Melissa.)* I was thirty-six years old. I could have gotten married again! I could have gotten married by a justice of the peace, or an Episcopalian, or a Methodist! But I didn't. I stayed Catholic. And what the hell for?
(A sudden burst of tears.)

My life — !
(She seizes control of herself.)

I invite you over here every Thursday for dinner and I thought you were my friend. I thought you were going to come to my defense, and you would prove that the Catholic Church was the one true Church, and that it's where I belong, and I made the right decision, and I even thought you'd go a way to convincing her how wrong she is. But you won't, because you won't lift a finger to help people like us. Well, if I'm going to hell, then I guess you won't want to come over here to dinner anymore. You probably don't want to be seen with someone like me. So let me give you back your stuff.
(She crosses to a shelf by the TV and starts roughly tossing DVDs at him.)

Here are your DVDs: *Keeping Up Appearances, Are You Being Served?, To the Manor Born, The Vicar of Dibley, Blackadder — Mr. Bean!* I hate that show! And I want my copy of *Angela's Ashes* back. You've had it for three years and I was too polite to say anything. There. I feel better already. I should have done this thirty years ago. And when you bring that book back, just leave it on the porch. No need dragging this out any longer than we have to. I just want to make a clean break. So, good night folks, and Father, it was nice knowing you. Have a nice life.

SCAB
Sheila Callaghan

More information on this author may be found on the "Meet the Authors" web page at www.smithandkraus.com.

Seriocomic
Anima, twenty-three

> *Anima is sitting in a bar, conversing to an unseen stranger. She is a little drunk, a little lost.*

ANIMA: What a piece of work is man, how noble in reason, how infinite in faculty, in form and move and inespresso ada-mahble . . . That's Shakespeare. I know more. I played Hamlet once in college. It was for a video project but I was good. No one could believe a chick Hamlet could be so goddamn good. Why not? Men played women's roles for years and years and years, no one had a problem. I made people CRY. Because I could *hear* them, assface. Sniff-sniff from behind me, honking into a hanky in front of me, wet gurgling noises on my right . . . That's a fucked-up feeling, you know? People who don't even know you, they believe so hard in your lie they make it their own. I'm not going to tell you my fucking name. I'm not here to get hit on. I'm just having a cocktail. *(She drinks.)*

An actor, really? Quite a rarity in these parts. No, I don't act anymore. I study. Eighteenth-century theater. No, Shakespeare was earlier. No, Tennessee Williams was later. No, Galileo was an astronomer. It's OK, everyone gets them mixed up. Get off me. My friend is picking me up. My roommate. My new roommate. She's brilliant. She's going to be a doctor soon. She analyzes women. Not a fucking shrink. She just does, then she makes history out of it.
(She drinks. A beat.)

No, but thanks. She'll be here any minute. Because I know. She takes care of me.

THE SECRET LIFE OF SEAGULLS

Henry Meyerson

More information on this author may be found on the "Meet the Authors" web page at www.smithandkraus.com.

Dramatic
Anne, early thirties

> *Anne is sitting on a beach. At this moment, confused about her suddenly falling apart life, she is talking to two uncomprehending seagulls, trying to figure things out.*

ANNE: I just need a little company. Feeling kind of down. You notice I just made a joke about feathers? Down, feathers? *(Beat.)* I'm thinking if I just talk, I might be able to figure out some stuff.

Not school stuff, like arithmetic, which I was always terrible at, but life stuff, like my husband and me, I? My marriage. That kind of stuff. *(Pause.)* Pretty here, isn't it? The blue sky, the white sands. Nice, you know. Peaceful. *(Pause.)* Well, I might as well be honest with you. I haven't been happy lately. Actually, it's been for a while. I think it's because I expected Don — that's my husband — I expect Don to be the answer for all my problems, and that may have been a problem itself. In other words, I think my answer was also my problem. That's confusing, isn't it? Maybe it's because he always held himself out to be my "little problem solver," my guardian. Maybe he just didn't want to do that anymore. I don't know. Come to think of it, I don't know too much about Don. I know he's kind of quiet, maybe a tad boring, but in a manly way, you know. Strong, silent, a tad boring Donny. Always dependable. *(Pause.)* I just realized I wanted to talk about me and I wound up talking about Don. Isn't that odd? What do you think that means? Don't tell anyone, but it's also a little odd I'm waiting for a seagull to answer me. Ha! That's funny. *(Beat.)* Anywhoo, Don left me and here I sit, alone with a couple of birds, trying to figure out what happened and what to do next. I mean, our marriage started out so beautifully. Bermuda honeymoon, nice house, good friends and now poof. The honeymoon is over. Still got the house and friends. I think I still have the house. I know I still have friends. Well . . . one for sure. In fact, that's her over there.

Sandy's her name. She is very nice, very supportive, you know. I think she's smarter than me. In fact, for all I know you guys are smarter than me. Are you two married? Never mind. *(Beat.)* Sandy thinks the problem is I'm dull. Do you think I'm . . . Never mind. I have to stop doing that. Silly me. But I am frightened, you know. I mean, what if Don decides to not come back. I can't just sit here the rest of my life talking to you guys. Not that there's anything wrong with you guys, but we don't share the same life experiences, do we? You're birds, I'm human. A very important difference and distinction, don't you agree?

SELF PHONE

Brendon Etter

More information on this author may be found on the "Meet the Authors" web page at www.smithandkraus.com.

Comic
Lily, eighteen to twenty-five

> *Lily is talking on her cell phone to her friend Hannah. She has just summoned the courage to sit down across the table from a man named Werner whom she doesn't really know but is trying to convince her of her charms. She reports her progress in her conversations with Hannah, preventing her from actually talking to Werner. This conversation gets out of hand, dwindling into recrimination and tears and causing Lily to invoke her goddess, Oprah, against Hannah.*

LILY: *(On cell phone.)* Hannah? Guess what!? I did it! Yes, totally . . . I said "Hi, my name is Lily" or something like that! Can you believe it?! I'm so excited! Yes! I know! I know! Where am I now? I'm sitting! I'm sitting in the other chair! I know! I don't know! I know! Yes . . . well, I just stepped up and sat in it! Yep, just sat right down! Ha-ha! I know! Ohh . . . I don't know? Should I be worried about that? Ahhh, too late, I'm worried about it now! Thanks a lot, Hannah! Why . . . why do you always do that? *(Starts getting huffy and a little teary.)* I meet someone, I introduce myself, and you have to ask me a question like that! No . . . no . . . I'm really mad right now! Yes, at you . . . well . . . come on! I never said that! I NEVER said that! No . . . no . . . I did NOT! I can't believe . . . you . . . but . . . I never . . . no . . . no . . . that's not what I said . . . I said . . . I said . . . will you listen to me? I said . . . I said that I just sat down . . . in the chair . . . I don't know, and I don't appreciate you bringing it up all the time . . . yes . . . yes . . . well, I FEEL like you bring it up all the time . . . yes . . . I do . . . you know how sensitive I am about that, and you bring it up all the time . . . and, yes, you do! You do! All the time, like you're trying to pick on me . . . you know, find the weakness like that one time on Oprah that girl said her best friend always knew her weaknesses, and she used them to control her like a puppet, like a puppet-friend, dancing on a string . . . and Oprah got really mad, and told her to stop it, and didn't she see that it was hurting her friend? And didn't she realize that it wasn't a real friendship if . . . if . . . one friend always held the strings . . . not real strings, but like fake strings that you can't really see but that the friend with the weaknesses CAN ALWAYS FEEL! And then Oprah told the friend with the fake strings that she needed to be her friend's friend in a real, no-strings, way . . . and then, do you remember what happened then . . . do you? Do you?! No?! Well, I do! Oprah wept! She wept, Hannah! Real tears like I'm crying right now! I don't want to be a puppet-friend! No! All right, then I'll answer your question, Hannah! No! OK!? No, I am not "smothering" him! No, it just started . . . our relationship . . . and it's very special, and I won't let you ruin it by making me worry if I'm smothering him! It's a beautiful relationship, Hannah! We are getting on just fine! Better than fine! So, stop the QUESTIONS!! All right?! All right!? Fine! Fine! GOOD-BYE! Yes! FOREVER!! GOOD-BYE INFINITY!! *(She hangs up and sits staring at the table and weeping openly.)*

SLOW FALLING BIRD

Christine Evans

More information on this author may be found on the "Meet the Authors" web page at www.smithandkraus.com.

Dramatic
Zahrah, thirty

> *Zahrah is an Iraqi refugee in an Australian immigration detention center in the desert, where asylum seekers are indefinitely detained under harsh conditions. Her husband and children have drowned en route to Australia; she is left alone with her newborn baby, who refuses to feed. She is about thirty, with a dry humor and a fierce desire to survive. Here, she tries to persuade her baby to feed and to face the new world they've landed in.*

ZAHRAH: Why smile when time hangs like a dead bird in a tree? Good question, shark baby. *(Beat.)*
I'll tell you what.
If you keep breathing, I will too. Just for now.
Do we have a deal? Look at that white sun. Go on, look right at it. Not a scrap of yellow in it. Blinding.
Go on, look at it.
Can't see it moving, can you? — I know you're looking — you're playing dead, but I can tell you're listening. Well, that sun is crawling down the sky's wall, like a fly. Yes it is. And when it sinks, this red fleapit will vanish and so will the guards — until they turn on the floodlights and start the head count. But in that little breath between day and night, well, this desert — the desert could be the sea. You know there are fish-bones in the desert, baby. From very long ago. And we can still see the stars, even older than the desert, tangled in the gridwire like jewels.
Your daddy loved the stars. But by the time your brothers were born there were no more telescopes. No more science, except for the science of killing. So, we'd sit out on the balcony after dinner and he'd smoke, and look up at the stars and tell your brothers stories. How long it took the light to reach us. How we're just a fleck of dust in the eye of history. Your brothers would [listen and ask] I can't do this.

Hear that, baby? That's the sound of wild dogs howling in the desert. I know it sounds scary but it's a good sign. Because . . . because we're still out at sea. But when you hear that sound of dogs howling, it means we've nearly landed. And when you wash up on shore it will be quiet at last. So very quiet. You can hear your own heart beating and the tide going out, taking the boat and all its water — ghosts with it. Yes, you're stranded all alone — but the sand's still warm as blood, like a blanket. And by the time you notice how far out the water's gone, you won't be thinking about who's drowned. Because by then, the wild dogs of this land will be all around you. And that's the time to smile, my baby. Smile and show your teeth.

See, this is your country now.

SLOW FALLING BIRD

Christine Evans

Dramatic
Joy, late twenties or early thirties

> *Joy is the shampoo-ad beautiful agoraphobic wife of Rick, a prison guard at an immigration detention center in the remote Australian desert. Joy moved from the city for Rick's job. She is isolated and desperately lonely and believes all their problems will be solved by having a baby. However, they have had no success in conceiving a child. Here, Joy whispers into the TV-glimmer darkness, trying to persuade the dream-child that haunts her to incarnate.*

JOY: I know you're out there. I can hear you crying sometimes.

Well, if you're watching — ta-da! *(Breaks a cigarette in half.)* See this? I'm doing penance, baby. These are coffin nails and I'm pulling them out of my skin. So you'll have a lovely clean bloodstream to nourish you when you attach. — If you attach.

I can't ask him to get tested. But the way things are going — I know you're out there, waiting.

See, the house is nice. It's waiting too. He comes home though, and the red dirt swirls in behind him, and then it's the six o'clock news. Strange to see your own town when the riots are on. The guards look like shiny insects in their shields. I liked it. I wanted him to bring his gear home. Can't ask though, he'd think that was kinky. I'm his blue-eyed girl. What color are your eyes, baby? Green, I'll bet. I freshen up for him, I put the air con on high, there's soothing classical music in the fridge, and the ceiling fan beats the whir of a cold beer, I never hear you when he's there, does that say something about us? And the shadows of the fan blades circle the room, like trapped and angry birds.

But they just circle, they don't land, there's beer in the oven, the air con is on freeze, he comes home and says he can't wake up, I don't see the problem with that but I can't ask what's that smell on your skin, like metal and something else, an animal smell, I'm not stupid, we don't talk about work, we just go to bed and rock towards you, circling like the shadows the ceiling fan makes and it just goes round and round and some days I never want to wake up. *(Beat.)* Sorry.

It's best to look forward. My doctor says that rumination is the main cause of depression which is why women. I listen and I nod but really what I think, is that hope is the main cause of depression. Because when it doesn't happen —

But this one thing. I can see so clearly.

A little baby white as milk, with eyes like a new suburb, empty of ghosts. I will find you.

And when I've found you we'll build our new house, brick by brick. And then.

We'll wall ourselves in.

Simple.

SOUL SAMURAI
Qui Nguyen

Dramatic
Lady Snowflake, twenties

> *Lady Snowflake is a samurai vampire who is confronting her former*
> *lover, Dewdrop, whom she feels left her to die in the streets five years*
> *earlier. Dewdrop has just killed Lady Snowflake's boss. They are now*
> *facing off on the Brooklyn Bridge near dawn.*

LADY SNOWFLAKE: Oh, I'm not, am I? I'm not the first girl you ever loved? The
first girl whose name you scribbled in your notebook with hearts circled
all around it? I'm not the first girl you ever let take you to heaven and back
with just the use of a tongue and a forefinger? What? Too graphic for you?
OK, how's this for PG-13? Am I not the first girl you left dying in the
streets five years ago because your chicken-shit ass wasn't brave enough to
open the goddamn car door to let me in? "Open the door. Open the fucking door." That meant for you to let me in, not for you to drive away, ya
dumb cunt. And secondly. Oh yes, bitch, there's a secondly. Secondly, to
follow up your utter failures at being my greatest love, it took you over a
half-decade to finally come back to get me some revenge. Shit, bitch, I got
cans of Spam that rot faster than that. And Spam, as you might know since
you're fucking Filipino and all, takes a goddamn long time to fucking rot.
You abandoned me, Dew. And the truth is, I'm glad I'm what I am now.
And not because of the superpowers or the amazing kinkilicious hot outfits. I'm glad 'cause if I weren't, that shit you done to me woulda hurt
pretty fucking bad. So, see, there's a boon to not having a soul, little Samurai. It makes living life a lot easier. Ain't that a something? But, worry not,
I'm not mad at ya. No way. You gave me a gift tonight after all. I'm the
new Kingsborough King. And it's all because of you. Let me look at you,
baby. I'm glad to be able to see that gorgeous face of yours again. That face
I once loved. A face that once loved me. You and I were meant to be
queens, baby girl. We were meant to rule the world, not stand here on this
old bridge fighting like a pair of some sad samurai. Let me give you what
you deserve. Oh, it's me. Every fine fiber, every delectable inch. I'm that
girl you loved and lost and now see again. And I'm asking you — girl who
once broke my heart — are you really going to kill me?

SOUTHERN RAPTURE

Eric Coble

More information on this author may be found on the "Meet the Authors" web page at www.smithandkraus.com.

Dramatic
Allissa, thirties-forties

> *Allissa is involved with a local theater that is putting on a production of* Rapture in America *(obviously, a doppelgänger for* Angels in America*). This has riled up the local right-wing Christian community, who have put pressure on the mayor not to let them do the play. Here, she is talking to the mayor about why he should not cave.*

ALLISSA: This morning my daughter looked up over her Eggo waffles and said to me: "Mommy, if I sing the wrong kind of song, will the police come and arrest me too?" . . .

Now I took this as a teachable moment, and I told her about the First Amendment and what happens in places where they don't have that sort of thing, and that led me to giving an overview of the Second World War, and I found myself describing in horrific detail the gas chambers at Bergen-Belsen to my six-year-old over waffles and hash browns all because you are afraid of some stupid gay fantasia! . . .

I want her to feel good about the city she is growin' up in. I want us all to feel good about it, and I want the nation to stop laughin' at us! Because I, for one, do not find this the least bit humorous!! . . .

I'm sorry. I'm exhausted. I was up early shredding my mother's newspaper. . . .

My point is, Winston, that I am not alone in these thoughts. There are a lot — many, many business leaders in the community who are speakin' to me, to my husband, who see you aren't returnin' their phone calls —

These are powerful people, Winston. They supported you for mayor because they felt you could take our city to the next level. If they come to feel they were misled in that belief . . . are you plannin' to run for reelection in a year and a half? . . .

I'm not threatening you. I am apprising you of a situation out there that you may not fully comprehend. I like you very much, Winston. I believe my family contributions show that. . . .

I'm not going to ask you to go back on your beliefs. But I will ask you if there's a way — a more subtle way than court orders and police arresting people — to make your point.

(She stands.)

That's all I'm askin' all of us. For us to rise to our best selves. Quietly.

TAKING FLIGHT

Adriana Sevann Nichols

More information on this author may be found on the "Meet the Authors" web page at www.smithandkraus.com.

Dramatic
Rhonda, thirties

> *Rhonda is in an intensive care unit when Adriana comes to visit her. Rhonda drifts off as she remembers the day Adriana took her to a botanica (a shop that sells herbs, amulets, and other items used in Afro-Caribbean religions and occult practices). She addresses the audience directly. A joyful memory book — ended by a heart monitor beeping and a life hanging in the balance.*

RHONDA: Adriana and I were goin' on this retreat called, "Celebrating the Goddess Within," and part of our homework was ta choose a goddess and start a relationship with her. So I didn't know what goddess ta pick. And I was talkin' ta Adriana about it, so she asks me, "What do I love most in nature?" So I tell ha, I love the sea. I'm from Oyster Bay, Long Island, and I've always loved the ocean. So she starts tellin' me about this goddess that her grandmother used to pray to called Yemaya. So Adriana takes me up to this place called a botanica. *(She laughs.)* We walk in and there is this weird lookin' creature behind the door — well I mean it wasn't alive or anything, but like this figure, made out of wood with co-conuts all around it and pennies and candles — *black* candles — which made me a little uncomfortable. It was a teeny tiny little place, but there was all this stuff for the money, health, good luck — it all felt a little hokey to me, you know, like a lot a voodoo tstchokas, but then we got to this section where they had all a this stuff of Yemaya, the goddess of the sea, and she is so beautiful. She has this really long dark hair and it looks like she has a bit of a tan. She's in this beautiful flowing white dress, nice figure, and her arms are open like . . . like she was calling me and when I looked at her I felt such peace that I knew I had found my goddess. So I got a Yemaya candle. A royal blue one to bring with me on the retreat. And they put some silver sparkles on it — I could choose between silver and gold — I chose the silver because I did not think the gold matched Yemaya's outfit. Adriana had chosen the goddess Oya *(She laughs.)* Oyaaaaa! I couldn't resist asking her if she was the goddess from Minnesota? So Adriana looks at me real serious like she does sometimes and she goes, "No. Oya is the goddess of the wind and the cemeteries. She's a warrior goddess symbolizing female power, righteous anger, and the storms of change!" You know Adriana can be so dramatic sometimes. So I said well OK honey, that sounds festive. So she got her burgundy-colored candle with everything on it and off we went — laughing and walkin' arm in arm down Amsterdam Ave. Oh!! They were filming *Law & Order* on the corner and we were trying to see Jesse Martin. I think he's so cute. And I was tellin' Adriana, "See, she shoulda been carrying around her headshots!" Cuz, I mean you never know, that coulda been a great opportunity for her.

We really had fun that day . . . the day I fell in love with Yemaya, the goddess of the sea.

THE THIRD STORY
Charles Busch

More information on this author may be found on the "Meet the Authors" web page at
www.smithandkraus.com.

Comic
Constance, thirties.

> *Dr. Constance Hudson is a frosty scientist in the 1940s who has devoted*
> *her entire life to her research, at the expense of all human relationships.*
> *In a rare vulnerable moment, she confides to her mentor, Dr. Hilda*
> *Rutenspitz, about a compelling fifteen-year-old girl she met while work-*
> *ing at a city health clinic years earlier.*

CONSTANCE: She was delicate, not particularly pretty, and excruciatingly shy. It took prodding for her to even reveal her name. Margaret. However, I sensed immediately that there was true intelligence hidden there. And this almost painful sensitivity. We barely exchanged a word and yet it was as if we were in perfect sympathy with each other. I thought, now this is someone I could help. Perhaps with her caring ways, she could grow up to be a nurse. Maybe even a doctor. And I would gain so much from knowing this child. The two of us. Margaret and me . . .

    I wrote them, explaining that I believed their daughter to be exceptional and wished to take her under my wing. It was a frustrating two weeks before I received a letter from her mother. She was grateful for my proposal and arranged for me to meet Margaret the following Saturday at Columbus Circle, at the edge of the park. I was nervous at the prospect of seeing her again, but Margaret surprised me by immediately kissing me on the cheek. A familiarity I found a tad excessive. I expressed that I would like very much to be her mentor. She thanked me profusely. She was remarkably outgoing and gregarious. So different from her reserved manner at the clinic. I apologize for the length of this anecdote. I'm not accustomed to telling stories. . . .

    Then I'll help myself to another Schnapps. It seems to make me more, um loquacious. For several months, Margaret came over at least four times a week. She was an excellent student and flourished under my

guidance. She was always full of good humor and physically demonstra-
tive. A hug around my waist, her head leaning against my shoulder . . .

Something kept me from returning her affection. There was a qual-
ity missing that I never saw again after that first meeting at the clinic.
The beautiful sadness. The poetic silence was gone. Late one afternoon,
we were discussing a paper she had written on Dostoyevsky's novella *The
Double*. The element of the book that seemed to haunt her was the
tragedy of two people sharing one identity.

TROJAN BARBIE

Christine Evans

More information on this author may be found on the "Meet the Authors" web page at www.smithandkraus.com.

Seriocomic
Polly X, fourteen

> *Polly X is a contemporary version of* Trojan Women's *Polyxena, who was Hecuba's daughter, sacrificed by the invading Greeks to Achilles to appease his ghost and bring wind after the sack of Troy. Here, she's a fretful, creative teenager stuck in a women's prisoner-of-war camp, trying to make sense of the fragments left of her city and her life after the invasion. She is dreaming into a future that can't see her back.*

POLLY X: Everything stinks here. I hate it. It stinks because we have to use gas for cleaning. Even the hospitals. For cleaning floors, toilets, wounds, everything. You can't get soap any more. And since the fence, you can't even go out. There's nothing to do. It's foul. This whole country is like a poisoned stinky gas station just waiting for someone to throw a match. I am sooo over it.

Oh, I want to smell desert rain again. It hasn't rained for three years. It's probably because we're cursed.

Anyway. Before the fence, Mama took me to the museum so I would see our "Cultural Heritage." But it was all looted, except for the Contemporary Art. So — we had to look at that instead. The program said that "Transcendent Ideas of Beauty" are no longer what art is about. But actually, I just think we can't afford it. Like I said, it's hard to get stuff. So most of it was really ugly, and all made of broken things. Or things that really aren't supposed to be art. Like bottles and rags and old shoes and stuff just stuck together.

The most disgusting sculpture of all was called TROJAN RAT. It had yellow eyes, and it was crouching in a pool of dark stuff that looked like oil, or blood, or something yukky. And it was hollow, you could see inside it because it was just made out of wire and plastic bags. Inside its belly it had a little white dining table, all tiny and perfect like real art. There was a family sitting round it, eating dinner.

But their house was bleeding and it was inside a rat.

Which had mean glittery eyes made of those yellow beer bottle tops that the soldiers leave lying around.

It made me feel sick but excited too.

I didn't like it but I did. I didn't but I did.

Mama hated it. She said it was "decadent and defeatist."

I said, Well Hecuba, we are defeated.

She didn't say anything to that.

And then I decided: I like Modern Sculpture.

On the way home, I started thinking about things I could make out of my own broken stuff. Mostly what I've got is these —
(Showing Barbie dolls.)

Most of them are a bit messed up, or they're covered in scribble and stuff.

Which is OK for Modern Sculpture.

I'm going to get a big piece of pink cardboard. Helen says if you're nice to the soldiers, they'll get you stuff. And then I'm going to get all my dolls and nail them on to it. In the shape of a big heart. So when it's finished, it will be this huge heart, made of smashed-up dolls. It will be sort of flat but sort of three dimensional. It will be very, very scary. I'm going to hang it out the front of the women's tents.

And I'm calling it TROJAN BARBIE. And when it's done, me and Cassandra will rain down revenge on our enemies! We will smash them like dolls! Death to the invaders!

TROJAN BARBIE
Christine Evans

Dramatic
Cassandra, sixteen

Cassandra is a contemporary version of the legendary Trojan princess to whom Apollo granted foresight — with the twist that she would never be believed. Here, she is full of the electric force of sexual awakening, which pours into her god-struck visions. There's an innocence to her, but her unpredictability gives her an air of danger.

(Cassandra has just had a vision of the abduction and attempted rape of her younger sister, Polly X [the previous scene in the play]. A captive herself, she is now reliving the moment of her own possession by Apollo and the dark vision it brought her.)

CASSANDRA: I think history's a wave. I think that's it.
It rolls and sucks at you and drags you under.
It smashes you into the future
right when you think you're on solid ground.
Like stepping on a landmine.

I like riding that wave. I like plunging my face in its foam.

My foaming-maned horse.
My Apollo. I stole him from the sea
he was drowning! I'm on the shore
watching him struggle — I know
the water's freezing
Too cold to survive
but there's a strong cord,
a cord like love
only darker, tying me to him
so I swim out to him
plunge my hands in his mane
drag him back to the shore. He sinks
to his knees

in the shallows and we're both
frozen — his heart's shuddering
like my teeth —

but then he bites me,
he won't let me go,
he gets over me and bites me
with his teeth on my neck
and nuzzles me with his soft
velvet mouth and then
he pushes his huge hot horse's cock into me
and I start to warm up . . . .

and then we're fucking
on the shoreline
where the waves churn into wet sand
and I'm crying because
I want to turn
into foam but I
want him more.

'Cause he's pointing a gun at me
and I'm moaning and pulling on the trigger.
And since then my belly has felt hot inside
like it's full of snakes. Something's growing in there.
Sometimes I hear the click of metal
when I walk
or the rasping of steel.

I think —
I think I'm pregnant with guns and bombs.
And the first man I'm with,
soon as he's in me —
that's it.
The world's going to blow.
I'm so happy I could die.

THE UNDERSTUDY
Theresa Rebeck

Seriocomic
Roxanne, thirties to forties

> *Roxanne is the stage manager of a Broadway production of a lost play*
> *by Franz Kafka. She is putting in a new understudy, who turns out to*
> *be a man she was going to marry who jilted her at the altar, never show-*
> *ing up and then disappearing. Here, she is explaining to one of the stars*
> *in the play what has made her so upset.*

ROXANNE: You know what I hate the most about it is how dumb the story
sounds. It's like an insult to my life, how without interest the whole "he
left her when she was practically walking down the aisle." You try telling
that story without sounding like a bad fucking romance novel, "jilted
when," and the endless moaning about, "the flowers!" "the caterers!"
"The invitations must have cost a fortune and then he just," all that
money that's all anyone could talk about because nobody wanted to talk
about my broken heart. It just reduces, everything, the internal story is
obliterated by the external facts in such a grotesque and to have the and
not just me, but the both of us, to have that annihilated in such a care-
less, because that's what, I'm telling you I can't even finish my sentences
that's how mad I still am about it. Because even if there was some question there, in him, some secret that could not enter the, that is only one
small piece, why should that secret become everything? The destruction
of everything? And with silence. Six years of silence. That is what I got.
He left without a word, not one word, and then there was nothing, and
then he was back, and of course I found out about it in the most hideous
way, I'm at an audition, and someone I barely know starts talking about
how she saw him at a reading, he's been back for months and no even,
nothing. Ever. He's back in the same city, he lives within miles of me and
there is no, what is it, why do people think silence is such a why is it a
choice? The failure of words. Yes words fucking fail us this is hardly news
but you TRY ANYWAY BECAUSE YOU'RE STILL ALIVE AREN'T
YOU. Silence is such a defeat. Yes I do know Kafka and I know the
whole story about him and Felice and I think Kafka is full of shit if you

want to know the truth. All those years he was supposedly in love with her and going to marry her but he just couldn't pull it off, could he? He dumps her to go off with Milena and Dora and all the other cute little literary groupies who were suddenly all hot for Franz Kafka because he was Mr. Literary Genius at the end, and there's Felice the whole time, when he's nobody, just loving him and ready to marry him and does she show up in even one of the novels? No. The only chicks who ever show up are like barmaids with whips. Oh and his sister, she gets to show up and throw an apple at him when he turns into a bug. I hate Kafka. Why do you guys think that not talking to us, like we're not even worth talking to, why is that such a great idea to you? I'm not crying. Stage managers do not cry. Stage managers just take care of things, so that you guys get to go out there and do all the — and you know what else, I was a fantastic actress. I was fucking genius. And let me tell you something, this play would be a lot better if there were some women in it. The law clerk couldn't be a woman? The land surveyor? The executioner? You know how good that scene would be if the executioner were a woman? It's written for fifteen different actors, Kafka didn't know anything about doubling. The producers got the bright idea that one giant movie star Bruce could play all the parts because they are alllll men. When it would be better, so many of these parts should be women! The guard, the judge especially she is just mean as a snake, hot and mean, all that shit she says about his "papers" being "limited," "this material is so limited," that is terrifying coming from a woman . . . "Limited. Constrained. Beneath contempt, my friend." My friend, so lame coming from a guy, but from a woman so much worse. Kafka's trying for terror? What scares men worse than a woman seething with dismissive rage?

UNUSUAL ACTS OF DEVOTION
Terrence McNally

More information on this author may be found on the "Meet the Authors" web page at www.smithandkraus.com.

Seriocomic
Josie, thirties to forties

> *A group of people who live in an apartment building have gathered together on the roof to celebrate the fifth wedding anniversary of a couple who live in the building. Josie, a bipolar English teacher recently returned from rehab, has had a little too much wine to drink.*

JOSIE: *(Finishes her glass of wine and pours herself another one.)* Number four, Mrs. Darnell! But who's counting? You've got the right idea: sleep: it's the most underrated human activity there is. Eating is great, sex used to be great (remember when sex was great, Mrs. Darnell?) — but even at their best — dinner at Antoine's or a really good bed partner (and God knows there were never many of them) — food and making love can't hold a candle to sleep. Nothing can hurt you when you're sleeping: you don't put on weight; there's no pressure to make anybody happy (including yourself) like when you're making love; and bad dreams — even the worst ones — are soon forgotten. Sleep is a lovely practice for death. The real thing won't be so bad when it comes along.
(She drinks some wine.)
But until then, I keep waking up to the same old ship. Shit. I said ship. I meant shit. Same old shit, same old shit. See? I can say it. This happens when I drink, if I'm not careful, Mrs. Darnell. My tongue gets thick. My defenses drop. I say lewd things. I do lewd things. I did a really lewd thing, the lewdest thing I ever did and I was stone cold sober. He told me he loved me. I told him he didn't have to say that. He said it anyway. I love you, Miss Shelton, I love you.
(She isn't finding anything in Leo's collection.)
There's never anything you want to play! Why is that?
(She gives up.)
I'd rather no music than music I don't really want. We can listen to the music of the city on a warm summer night. Ssssh! Listen. There is so

much to hear if you just stay quiet and listen for it.

(She stands at the parapet and looks out. We listen to the city with her for a while.)

You know what I like most about New York? You can be completely anonymous here. No ones care who you are but you, what you do but you, who you inappropriately fuck but you.

WHAT ONCE WE FELT

Ann Marie Healy

More information on this author may be found on the "Meet the Authors" web page at www.smithandkraus.com.

Dramatic
Cheryl, late twenties to early thirties.

> *Cheryl is speaking to her sick and dying mother. She is recounting the story of running into a privileged Keeper at her border-crossing job and expressing her frustration over her own disenfranchised situation as a Tradepack. (Keepers are the healthy, elite members of society, and Tradepacks are the sick, weak members.)*

CHERYL: A
Keeper
Came through my line today
You should have seen her
Mom
You should have seen her
Attitude
Back in the day
Before The Transition
She wouldn't have dared
She said
When she left
Do you know what she said?
Mom?
(No response. Knitting knitting. Knitting knitting.)
She said *Ta Ta*
She said *Ta Ta* and
She told me about
Some bistro or some
Some some dinner that would change her life
Something
She said she was going to a dinner that would change her life
And I said

Fine you can go
Something something
(Pause. Knitting Knitting. Knitting Knitting.)
Change your life
Change your life
I didn't even know bistros
Still existed
I didn't know
You could just go to a dinner
A bistro
And change your life
(Franny quietly moans in pain. She is essentially unconscious with pain.)
Oh
Oh no
Oh no I'm so sorry
Please stop
They won't give us more pills
You know that don't you
I would do anything
But I —
(Cheryl tries to resume her knitting. She knits she knits she knits to control
her rage. Franny moans with more quiet agony.)
Oh Mom
Oh Mom please
No shhhhh No No
(She holds Franny like a baby.)
No no
Shhhhhhhhh
Shhhhhhhhh
It's going to be just fine
I'm so sorry
So so sorry
I'm
I'm
Ta ta
I can't stop hearing her voice
In my head
Ta ta
Ta ta

Over and over
I hear her say it
(Cheryl is crying silently with rage.)
Ta ta
She said
Ta ta
Change your life
Change your life
Ta ta
Why do you get to change your life?

WHAT ONCE WE FELT

Ann Marie Healy

Dramatic
Joan, thirties to fifties

> *Joan, a prison guard, is speaking to Cheryl in her cell. Cheryl has just killed her sick and suffering mother in an act of mercy. Joan is trying to convince her to join an underground resistance group she is starting to get more equality and justice for the Tradepacks (the sick and weak members of society).*

JOAN: I'm supposed to take away these needles you know
Seeing as you used 'em as weapons
OK? OK?
(Joan pauses to consider the safety of what she is about to offer before leaning in.)
You helped us
Do you know that?
Your desperation: your anger
Your story's giving us the courage to get organized:
The Resistance is finally getting organized
We're not gunna take this
We do not have to take this
(She slides her a little card cautiously.)
I'm getting together all of the groups.
We're all underground
We're all hush hush
But soon
Very soon:
There are gonna be marches
There are gonna be protests
We're protesting because of you:
You: your Mama
Your story
You have no idea how much strength your story has given us.
(She looks at Cheryl, trying to assess if she can hear the following.)

You can't just act once
And shut your eyes
And go to sleep
You gotta act
Every day
Every day honey
Every day
(Another gesture of comfort.)
When you're ready
You dial this number and ask for Joan

WHAT ONCE WE FELT

Ann Marie Healy

Dramatic
Yarrow, forties to fifties

> *Yarrow is speaking to her partner, Benita, about deciding whether or not to follow through on a pregnancy with a child that might be severely sick or disabled (in the world of the play, such people are labeled Tradepacks).*

YARROW: Oh
   Well sorry
   Oh God
   Are you going to start crying?
   Don't start
   OK good
   Well I won't tell you how to think
   But if you think this way
   You shouldn't all right
   Don't think this way
   It's
   Dangerous
   It's misguided
   We're in an *ideal* situation so why would we
   Open
   This
   This
   Pandora's Box
   It's *an Error*
   We have no idea what that means
   Why would we
   When we don't —
   Desperate people make these kinds of decisions
   We are not desperate
   We have choices //
   That's all
   No

No I refuse to let you
Get romantic and Airy
Fairy
I will make you
See the real
The real
Situation as it stands
And that means —
What if
What if
It's a Tradepack
This Error
We don't know
Error could mean
Tradepack
And if it's a *Tradepack*
What
What then?
What will you do if it gets sick?
You take care of her
Day and night
And what do you get in return?
All day all night
You don't get shit
You might not get smiles
You might not get fingers //
You might not get
Who knows?
You have NO IDEA

WORSE THINGS

Mona Mansour

More information on this author may be found on the "Meet the Authors" web page at www.smithandkraus.com.

Dramatic
Liz, early thirties

> *Liz speaks to her girlfriend/partner, Maeve. They've been together for a few years, and while Maeve loves to process endlessly about the relationship, analyzing each and every minutia of feeling, Liz quite frankly finds this a buzz-kill. This piece comes right after they started to fool around but got stopped by some tidbit Maeve wanted to analyze, and Liz told Maeve she'd rather talk about anything — ethnic cleansing, even — than their relationship.*

LIZ: I just don't want to spend all our time talking about our sexual enjoyment. Every day, every WEEK we spend time talking about our shit, our SEXUAL shit, whether we can fully relax or not. Why, why not, what it means to completely GIVE IN, why we feel we can't, why we need to have time BEFORE, but not AFTER — before because we need the tonal change, the tonal shift, into sex. And it's hard, because this world is fucked up and you get pushed in this world, just to go out and buy soy milk or whatever can be a trial, and you have to wear sunglasses to protect, to see out but not let them see *in*, my God —

and in fact this same protective covering is what we need to let go of when it's time to FUCK, be fucked, etc., and I gotta be careful not to use that word at the WRONG time with you because some days it just hits you as dirty, the whole thing, and fuck or be fucked sounds either (a) crass or (b) like I'm just this suburban person, this actually asexual person trying to BE sexual and therefore (b1) that's even worse, because what's worse than an actual asexual, nonsexual, nonsexed person using words like fuck, and so on? Nothing. I'm made needy, I'm made dirty, by saying that word. God I'm sick of myself.

YOO-HOO AND HANK WILLIAMS

Gregory Moss

Comic

Amy, midtwenties to early forties

Amy is speaking to her newly adopted cat, Huey, who will not come out from under the couch. She's lonely, single, can't seem to find human companionship, and now even this cat won't get close to her. It's evening, and Amy's just gotten home from work.

AMY: Huey?

Huey?

Huey for God's sake!

Huey come here.

Huey, I just — I just want to talk to you, Huey. Come here.

Huey, will you please come out from under there and just come over here and talk to me, you stupid cat?

(Sighs. Sits.)

Coo coo? Meow-meow? Kiss-kiss?

(Beat.)

You peed on my favorite skirt and I didn't even get mad. Huey! I am so good to you! I am like your best friend, Huey, in the world! You don't even have anyone but me!

But you know what?

I don't even want you, Huey.

I don't.

My mother made me take you when she got her new couch.

I never wanted you.

I don't want a cat!

(Beat.)

I do want a cat.

— But I want a different cat, Huey!

I want a cat that's gonna play wth me and sit on my lap.

That's your job, Huey.

I want a cat that's gonna take me out for picnics by the river and dinner at fancy restaurants and who'll pay for me at the movies and hold the door to let me in.

I want a cat that's handsome and tall with big hands and black hair and a black leather jacket and looks like Robert Mitchum but talks like Marlon Brando and who'll walk through the door and make my mom have a fatal HEART ATTACK!

I wanna run through the house screaming and knocking everything down — tear the plastic covers off the furniture!

And jump on your motorcycle and take off across Texas and Arizona and drive all night every night nonstop with the hot desert wind coming through our hair and me and you we just — FUCK like crazy rabbits without stopping! We don't even pull over, just keep going, me on your lap, pushing on the accelerator, the roads empty and the bike going faster and faster and the moon above smiling and nodding, cheering us on, telling us "HELL YES!"

(Beat.)

That's the kind of cat I want, Huey.

And you don't really do anything like that.

Do you. Huey?

(Beat.)

Huey, if you are shitting or something, I will kill you.

(Beat.)

I have a pretty red dress. I get my hair done. I take care of myself.

I have a voice. I have a body.

I can't see any of it.

I have nothing to do with them.

Sometimes, when I'm alone, I don't even know if I am there.

(Beat.)

I think, if someone were to touch me — I would know then what I look like.

What my shape is.

It would prove it.

If he were to kiss me,

then I would know I have lips.

If he whispered in my ear,

I would know then, that I can hear.

If he touched my skin,

I would know then

That I am here.

(Pause.)

I clean up after you, and feed you, and you're supposed to love me.

That's the agreement.

You love me.

(Beat.)

You love me.

SCENES

THE CHERRY SISTERS REVISITED
Dan O'Brien

Comic
Effie, eighteen
Addie, nineteen
Lizzie, twenty-three
Jessie, thirty-two

> *This scene takes place in a barn, in winter, on the Cherry family farm in Marion, Iowa, circa 1890. The girls are planning and rehearsing their takeover of vaudeville. (Note: The characters are all young women; their specific ages aren't important.)*

EFFIE: Here's what I envision:

Numerous acts, some funny, some sad. Some songs, Lizzie, you'll sing a few pretty ditties. Something sentimental of the euphemistic school. You know the score. I have the titles, you can fill in the rest.

One: *I Ain't Never Been Kissed.* Two: *Let's Canoodle in the Doodle-ee-doo.* And three — *Corn Juice!* Exclamation point. Naturally.

Let me write this all down :

(She does, in a little brown book that seems to appear in the ether.)

ADDIE: Where'd you find that?

EFFIE: In the ether.

JESSIE: *(Eating cheese.)* You're nuts, Effie Cherry . . .

EFFIE: What's nuts? to dream? — Perchance to dream, Jessie!

LIZZIE: Who said that?

ADDIE: Walt Whitman.

LIZZIE: Who's he?

ADDIE: Some nurse.

LIZZIE: How's this sound?

(Lizzie sings, with her ukelele:)

LIZZIE: Let's canoodle in the doodle-ee-doo
And foodle with the poodle-ee-pee.
I'll piddle your diddle
If you fiddle my middle,
Canoodling in the doodle-ee-doodle-ee-doodle-ee Dum-m-m!

EFFIE: Keep working on that one.

We'll need some playlets —

LIZZIE: What's a "playlet"?

ADDIE: Like a play, but suckling.

LIZZIE: — That's a good one, Addie!

ADDIE: Is it? I don't know about that one yet . . .

EFFIE: And some comic monologuing. Addie, that's your forte, make it fresh, make it funny.

JESSIE: — What about me?

EFFIE: What about you, Jessie.

JESSIE: What do I do?

EFFIE: Well, so far. I've got you down for the. . . "heavy lifting." Jessie.

(Pause.)

JESSIE: Lifting what?

EFFIE: Props and scenery, mostly.

LIZZIE: You're the most athletic, Jessie. Everyone knows that . . .

JESSIE: What about Addie? — she's got man-hands!

(Addie examines her hands.)

LIZZIE: It's true . . .

JESSIE: I'm heavy . . . if that's what you mean . . . I don't eat much. Lord knows we don't *ever* eat much, any of us, except maybe cheese, on a good day. . . . Corn . . . It's a mystery to me. I'm just naturally matronly . . .

(Jessie eats some more cheese.)

JESSIE: — But I can't lift much! My heart's not strong. Like Momma's wasn't . . .

(A deep pause, surprisingly felt. They all glance at, or away from, or just think about Effie and her very large head. Effie touches said head, without noticing what she's doing. Addie changes the subject:)

ADDIE: So I'm reading this book:

(Shows the cover.)

LIZZIE: *So You Want to Live in Vaudeville?* *(Pause.)* Well do you?

ADDIE: It's a rhetorical question. It's got killer Brooklynese.

EFFIE: Definitions?

ADDIE: You betcha.

EFFIE: Phonetic?

ADDIE: No, English.

LIZZIE: Where is Phoenicia, anyway?

EFFIE: Let me hear some please:

ADDIE: "Take my seat, young goil! I'm only goin' so far as Yahnkers!"
  (Pause. Effie savors:)
EFFIE: That's beautiful.
ADDIE: Isn't it?
LIZZIE: Where is Yonkers anyway?
ADDIE: Brooklyn, I guess.
JESSIE: That's crude. I think such speech is vulgar.
LIZZIE: What about a Negro song? Some kind of sassy soft-shoeing? Some
  blackface maybe? Addie would make a very convincing coon, I think.
JESSIE: That is also in poor taste.
LIZZIE: Whose taste? I find their music stirring.
JESSIE: In the twentieth century no one will laugh at Negroes.
LIZZIE: Why not? Where will they have all gone?
ADDIE: The twentieth century is eight years from now, Jessie . . .
JESSIE: I know that. — This is *America*, Addie!
EFFIE: And when our act is strong and tight we'll do a show, at home, at the
  Marion Grange Hall. We'll hone our craft on friendly turf, then raise
  enough in capital to take our show all the way to Cedar Rapids —
  (Lizzie gasps.)
EFFIE: Don't gasp, it's true — it's within our reach, our grasp. Every day, a
  great actress dries up onstage, like a prune, and every day another one
  blooms!
JESSIE: But what if we're not good enough . . . ?
  *(A sudden, long pause ensues. Jessie eats some more cheese, morosely. Effie's
  about to touch her head again, but Addie takes her hand and holds it.)*
LIZZIE: He looked so sad in that coffin, the earth was frozen six feet down . . .
  (Jessie eats more cheese.)
EFFIE: We'll need a name.
JESSIE: What for?
EFFIE: Our act, of course.
ADDIE: We have one already, don't we?
LIZZIE: Do we? Which one?
JESSIE: The name God gave us.
ADDIE: You mean Pops gave us . . .
LIZZIE: "The Cherries."
  (It just sits there in the barn.)
ADDIE: We'll be popular with the men.
LIZZIE: Why?
JESSIE: Yes, why, Addie?

ADDIE: Where's Ella with our lunch?

LIZZIE: I'm hungry now too . . .

JESSIE: Have my cheese.

(She offers Lizzie some.)

LIZZIE: I've got to watch my figure. *(Pause.)* We all do.

JESSIE: *(Eating more cheese.)* We all do what?

EFFIE: What's wrong with our figures, Lizzie?

LIZZIE: Well. With the possible exception of you, Effie, who's already bone
thin, like a thin old swayback mule —

EFFIE: Like a what?

LIZZIE: — the rest of us are far too . . . matronly. *(Pause.)* Like Jessie said.

EFFIE: How can we be matronly? we're not even married —

LIZZIE: That's my point exactly.

It hardly matters much for you, Addie — you're the funny one, all
that matters is your wits. If you get fat you'll be *more* funny, probably,
because fat people are mostly jolly, except when they're mean, and then
they're positively evil . . .

And as for Effie it's her brains inside that great big head of hers
And Jessie here is for the heavy lifting, as we've discussed, despite the
danger to her heart.

No: I'm the one who must stay pretty, Pops would always say.

ADDIE: Where's Ella with our gosh-darned lunch!

JESSIE: Such language!

EFFIE: She's inside sewing our new leotards.

JESSIE: Are you sure that's such a good idea?

ADDIE: Some of history's best seamstresses have been mentally impaired.

LIZZIE: Really?

ADDIE: No, I was just trying out a joke — does it work?

JESSIE: I don't think she should be let loose out there, what with all this wind
and driving snow . . .

EFFIE: She's not a cat.

ADDIE: It *is* snowing fiercely out there, Effie . . .

EFFIE: It's always snowing here.

LIZZIE: I know. Why *is* that?

EFFIE: We need to focus, girls! — Focus! We've got so much more work to do!

LIZZIE: I think I see her coming now . . .

JESSIE: That's her outside in the wind and driving snow — keep walking, Ella!
You can make it!

LIZZIE: Are you sure that's Ella out there in the wind and . . . ?

JESSIE: Driving snow.

LIZZIE: Driving snow?

JESSIE: Who else could she be?

LIZZIE: I don't know, a ghost maybe?

ADDIE: Whose ghost?

LIZZIE: She looks a lot like Momma did . . .

JESSIE: Do you remember when Momma would take the washing from the line, in the snow? The temperature would drop, and the snow would sweep in . . . The sheets would be frozen, they'd crack like boards when she folded them in front of the fire.

EFFIE: — What about: "The Beautiful Cherry Sisters"?

(They look each other up and down.)

EFFIE: No.

ADDIE: That won't work.

LIZZIE: — *I'm* not ugly!

ADDIE: That's mostly true.

EFFIE: "The Four Cherry Sisters" simply?

LIZZIE: "The Four Cherry Sisters Simply" is far too modest.

JESSIE: Five. With Ella.

(Another pause.)

JESSIE: Well we have to, don't we? We can't leave her alone out here, surely . . .

ADDIE: Can she sing and dance?

JESSIE: She's one of us, Addie, she's a Cherry!

ADDIE: She's an idiot, Jessie. *(Short pause.)* I mean that in the clinical sense.

JESSIE: So?

EFFIE: People are going to laugh at her . . .

LIZZIE: But that's the point, isn't it?

JESSIE: — Come on, Ella! You can make it!

LIZZIE: She's teetering in the wind!

JESSIE: She's fallen off the trail!

LIZZIE: She's carrying our new leotards — they're pretty! They're bunched before her face!

JESSIE: Look — one's flown away!

LIZZIE: Like a flamingo!

JESSIE: Do you remember how silent mother was? How graceful and composed . . . ?

LIZZIE: Like Ella, though not as dumb. . . .

JESSIE: I remember her standing at the stove, with baby Addie in her arms, rocking her to sleep and singing . . . She had such a pretty voice, like you do, Lizzie . . . with her breast in Addie's mouth . . .

ADDIE: I wish I could remember that.

EFFIE: — You were too young when she died, Addie.

ADDIE: What do you know — you weren't even fully born yet!

(Addie immediately regrets what she's said.)

JESSIE: — Keep walking, Ella, you're almost here!

LIZZIE: Oh look — she's fallen in a drift —

ADDIE: Oh now she's up again! Here she comes!

EFFIE: — "The Musical Cherries"?

LIZZIE: Redundant.

EFFIE: "Cherries A-Poppin'!"

JESSIE: Been done before.

EFFIE: "The Five Ripe Cherries"?

ADDIE: That sounds like we smell bad.

LIZZIE: Or taste good.

ADDIE: That's filthy!

JESSIE: — It doesn't matter what we're called, girls! No one's going to care! No one's going to believe us, when they see us up there on that stage at the Marion Grange Hall. They'll say, Who do these girls think they are? We knew their poor mother, we knew Pops — we know what he was like . . . No, they won't believe us for a minute.

EFFIE: Then we'll have to believe it first. *(Pause.)* If we believe it, then they will.

JESSIE: Is that how it works . . . ?

EFFIE: What do you say, girls? Can you believe it?

(No one answers. The answer would seem to be "maybe"?)

EFFIE: That's it: "The Unbelievable Cherry Sisters!" *(Pause.)* Exclamation point!

JESSIE: Well it's accurate, anyway . . .

THE GOOD NEGRO
Tracey Scott Wilson

Dramatic
Corinne, thirties
James, thirties

James is a charismatic civil-rights leader modeled on Dr. Martin Luther King Jr. He has been caught philandering, and here, his wife confronts him about it.

(Corinne and James at home.)

CORINNE: I thought it was going to be one of your sermons. *(Pause.)* I been saving the sermons people send me in the mail. *(Pause.)* Say you're sorry James. Say you're sorry. Say you're sorry. *(Pause.)* Every time somebody goes after you or tries to hurt you I feel it in my body. Right now, all I want to do is hurt you and I don't feel anything. *(Pause.)* Is that why you won't let me travel with you?

JAMES: No, no, no.

CORINNE: Because I thought it was because —

JAMES: It's dangerous. Somebody has to be here for the kids if something —

CORINNE: Uh-uh.

JAMES: — happens to me.

CORINNE: Don't do that now. Don't put that death mess on me. You want me to feel sorry for you?

JAMES: They manipulated things to make them sound worse.

CORINNE: So you never fucked anybody else then?

JAMES: They're trying to destroy me Corinne.

CORINNE: You give them the bullets. *(Pause.)* I didn't mean to say bullets.

JAMES: I've made some mistakes.

CORINNE: Mistakes? *(Beat.)* That Sullivan woman on there.

JAMES: No, no, no. I . . . That's one of the things they manipulated. I did not. Absolutely not.

CORINNE: I shook her hand, kissed her cheek, said, "have your daughter come around and play with the kids."

JAMES: Corinne, listen. I'm telling you.

CORINNE: Do you laugh about it? I heard a lot of laughing on that tape. Is that what you're laughing about? Me? Your ugly, stupid wife.

JAMES: Don't say that. Please. Don't talk like that.

CORINNE: I do my job Jimmy. Don't I? What am I doing wrong? Tell me.

JAMES: You're perfect Corinne. Just perfect. All right? But sometimes I just can't think straight and I go with these other women.

CORINNE: And these other women help you think straight?

JAMES: No, that's not . . . I'm afraid. I'm afraid I'll be alone when they take me, alone in my bed, some hotel room somewhere. I don't want to die alone Corinne.

(James reaches out to Corinne.)

JAMES: I'm sorry Corinne. I am so, so sorry. *(Silence.)* I love you.

(She pulls away.)

CORINNE: You love me? Screaming out some other woman's name? Saying those nasty things. I wish I could go out there and do any damn thing I wanted. But I can't. I can't. How do you? How do you pray after committing all that sin? How do you call yourself a minister, Jimmy? I don't understand. You love me? What?

JAMES: That's not me on there. Those things on there. That's not who I really am Corinne. It doesn't mean —

CORINNE: How am I going to get this out of my head Jimmy? How am I going to go on now ignoring things? Pretending you're not a dog?

JAMES: Don't let that tape destroy us Corinne. That's what they want. That's why they sent it.

CORINNE: You're destroying us Jimmy. You! Not anybody else. You! That's why this movement is all messed up 'cause you all messed up. Screwing your congregation, rubbing up against everything that moves. Acting just like the coons they say we are.

JAMES: OK. We just need to —

CORINNE: Please stop it. will you stop it please.

JAMES: I will. I will. I will. I will. I will.

(Pause.)

CORINNE: I don't want them shaking my hands when they come to the meetings. I don't want them smiling in my face saying, "hey, hey, Mrs. Lawrence, I'm praying for you. Stay strong." You ass. Tell them James. Don't touch. Don't speak to my wife.

JAMES: I promise you. I will never stray again. This is God's warning. And I will never stray again. *(Beat.)* I got lonely, traveling so much.

CORINNE: I got lonely too James. All the time. *(Beat.)* All the time.

(James reaches out to Corinne.)

CORINNE: But there's no tape of me out there is there?

IPHIGENIA

Don Nigro

Seriocomic
Lexie, twenty
Jenna, nineteen

A room in a church in Armitage, a small town in the hilly part of east Ohio, in 1910. Jenna appears in her wedding dress. Lexie is trailing her, putting in last-minute pins in the back. Jenna and Lexie Ryan are sisters, daughters of Michael Ryan, the local bank president. Jenna is nineteen, Lexie a year younger, although Lexie has always seemed the more mature of the two, while Jenna is beautiful, dreamy, and strange. Lexie has a sharp tongue, but she loves her sister, although it bothers her that all the boys have always fallen in love with Jenna. Both girls adore their father, but are frustrated by his apparent inability to express affection. It's Jenna's wedding day. She's going to marry Nick, thirty, a handsome and somewhat wicked young man who's shown up in town and inexplicably been given an important job at the bank by their father. Jenna believes Nick is blackmailing Michael for something buried deep in the past and has accepted Nick's proposal in an attempt to sacrifice herself for her father. She has mixed feelings about Nick. So does Lexie. In this scene, just before the wedding, some of the buried tension between the sisters is finally coming out. The Thomas they speak of is their younger brother.

JENNA: Ouch. Stop it.

LEXIE: Hold still.

JENNA: You're sticking me with pins.

LEXIE: Do you want your dress to fall off?

JENNA: I want you to stop sticking pins in my butt. I'm going to get blood poisoning. Do I look all right?

LEXIE: *(Pulling her roughly back.)* If you don't hold still I'm going to knock you unconscious with that big crucifix over there.

JENNA: If I don't look all right, tell me the truth.

LEXIE: Jenna, you look amazing. You always look amazing. You'd look amazing wearing a potato sack and a bucket on your head. Men will fall dead at your gaze. Women will eviscerate themselves in the vestibule with uncontrollable jealousy. Now, hold still, or I'll make sure you don't live to enjoy your wedding night.

JENNA: It isn't real. I'm not really getting married. It's all some sort of nightmare. I'll wake up and we'll be children again, playing in the street with Tom and the Rose girls. They're here, aren't they? Are the Rose girls here?

LEXIE: They're all here. Everybody's here. Half the county is here. I didn't know there were this many people in Ohio.

JENNA: Lexie?

LEXIE: Don't move.

JENNA: *(Holding still for her.)* I'm doing the right thing, aren't I?

LEXIE: Of course you're not.

JENNA: Don't make fun of me. I can't deal with that today.

LEXIE: I'm perfectly serious. He's a scoundrel and he's going to make you miserable.

JENNA: He is, isn't he?

LEXIE: He absolutely is. But then, everybody ends up miserable anyway. And he's a good-looking scoundrel, at least. Good in bed. At least he is in my fantasies. I imagine that makes up for a lot.

JENNA: Lexie. Do you hate me?

LEXIE: Of course I hate you. I've always hated you. I'm your sister. That's my job.

JENNA: You like him.

LEXIE: I don't like him at all. Nobody does, except Thomas, and he's a moron.

JENNA: You like him a lot more than I do.

LEXIE: He makes my flesh crawl. He's a horrible, horrible person. Are you happy?

JENNA: If you think he's horrible then why do you sit on the porch and talk to him for hours?

LEXIE: There. All done. Let me look at you.

JENNA: And when you get up and go in the house, it always seems to me he's disappointed, to be left alone with me. And he never has anything to say to me. It's you he talks to.

LEXIE: He talks to me because you don't say anything.

JENNA: I don't know what to say to him. I don't know why he wants to marry me. I don't even think he does want to marry me. I think he'd rather have you.

LEXIE: If he wants me, why is he marrying you?

JENNA: I don't know. I don't understand it. I don't understand anything about him.

LEXIE: Stop trying to make sense out of him. He's a man. He's got the brain of a lizard.

JENNA: No he doesn't. He's very smart. He's just —

LEXIE: What? He's what? Tell me what he is, Jenna. I'd very much like to be enlightened about that. Because I've been trying hard to figure out just what the hell he is, and I still haven't got a clue.

JENNA: I don't want you to be unhappy.

LEXIE: Well, then, you'd better kill me, because that's what people are, when they're alive. Maybe we get to be happy when we're dead, but I doubt it.

JENNA: Some people are happy.

LEXIE: Only the ones who aren't paying attention.

JENNA: I just want to say, you're doing a wonderful job of cheering me up on my wedding day.

LEXIE: Oh, is that what I was supposed to be doing? Maybe I didn't read the old maid sister handbook carefully enough. He wants you. You're what he wants. God only knows why, but that's clearly the way it is. And if he wants you, and you want him, then the two of you probably deserve each other, in some thoroughly twisted way I'll never understand, so there's no good reason why the both of you shouldn't be any more miserable than any other married people, as long as you don't pay too much attention to each other. That's the real secret of being married, I think: learning how to ignore the other person as much as possible. Otherwise, you'll rip each other apart like weasels in a bag.

JENNA: You're in love with him.

LEXIE: I'm not stupid enough to be in love with anybody.

JENNA: Lexie —

LEXIE: Do you love this person?

JENNA: You're not stupid enough to love anybody, but you think I am?

LEXIE: Essentially, yes. If you love him, then what's the problem? And if you don't love him, why are you marrying him?

JENNA: It feels like the right thing to do.

LEXIE: That's a terrible reason to do anything. Trying to do the right thing kills more people than lightning and hunting accidents combined. How can it be the right thing to marry a man you don't even like?

JENNA: It's possible for married people to be happy. Mother and Father are happy, aren't they? Sort of?

LEXIE: Mother and Father don't even know each other.

JENNA: They know each other. They've been married for twenty years.

LEXIE: That proves it. A long marriage is only maintained in a state of profound ignorance on the part of one or both parties.

JENNA: Lexie, you're not helping me.

LEXIE: You don't need my help. You've got your husband. He'll help you. He'll be glad to help you out of this dress, that's for sure.

(Pause.)

Look. If you don't want to marry him, then don't.

JENNA: I've got to marry him.

LEXIE: Why?

(They look at each other. Jenna is about to say something when there's a knock on the door. They both look at the door.)

OOHRAH
Bekah Brunstetter

Dramatic
Sara, early thirties
Abby, late twenties

> *Sara and Abby are sisters. It is morning, in the kitchen of Sara's new home. Sara's husband, Ron, has just returned on his fourth tour from Iraq and is having a lot of trouble readjusting to domestic life. Sara is drowning these frustrations by avoiding them and focusing all efforts toward a birthday party for her daughter, Lacey, who has recently given up dresses for guns and combat boots. Abby, engaged to her longtime civilian boyfriend, has just had a torrid late-night encounter with a mysterious marine. (Note: A backslash [/] indicates where the next line of dialogue overlaps the current one.)*

(The kitchen. Sara is taking wine glasses out of their Target boxes, lining them up neatly on the table. Abby walks in, fresh from sleep, with a huge smile on her face. She goes for coffee.)

SARA: *(Not looking at her.)* Chris's called three times just this morning.

ABBY: I'll see him later, we're going to look at pillows or something. *(She sits at the table.)* Where's Lacey?

SARA: She went to Home Depot with Ron, he's getting stuff for the living-room carpet. And maybe lookin' at a new dishwasher for me. And maybe a ficus plant for the hall. He's doin' real well, Ron is.
    Your new friend was gone before I even woke up.

(Abby smiles, hard, into her coffee. Sara sees this.)

SARA: What the hell are you smiling like that for?

ABBY: Nothing.

(Abby looks at the wine glasses.)

SARA: *(Proudly.)* They're for Lacey's party Sunday. Ron got 'em, he got up early this morning and went to Target and got all sorts of stuff for the house.

ABBY: So You're gonna get the kids drunk?

SARA: For the PARENTS. That one's for white wine, and these're for red, and these're for sherry which I think is dessert wine. They're just like the ones they use in Tuscany like in *Under the Tuscan Sun.*

You hold 'em at the base and swish it around and the wine breathes, 'cause apparently wine's gotta breathe too.

ABBY: Since when do you drink wine?

SARA: I don't know. Since I want a complete kitchen, and the / parents —

ABBY: All right.

SARA: And for dinner parties.

ABBY: Since when do you have dinner parties?

SARA: I'm waitin' 'til my kitchen's complete, Damn!

ABBY: OK, OK! Geez louise. Not sleep good?

SARA: I slept fine, did you?

ABBY: Yeah.

SARA: On the couch? The whole night?

ABBY: Yeah, on the couch.

SARA: Ron thinks it best that you go on and find yourself your own place to live. Me, I don't care, I don't mind, I like havin' you here but Ron —

ABBY: Wait — what?

SARA: I mean, it's not the biggest house in the world — walls're thin, and we need our privacy, you know? I'm only in my middle thirties and I have — sexual — needs, and so does Ron.

ABBY: So because he says so, I gotta go?

SARA: Not JUST / because —

ABBY: You always do whatever he wants!

SARA: You just shouldn't have done that in my *house,* Abby. This is *my* house. I don't want Lacey bein' around that stuff.

ABBY: What stuff?

SARA: Just — Why don't you just move in with Christopher?

ABBY: 'Cause, cause, we're getting married, and then we'll get our own place. His place now's too small and his underwear is everywhere. I don't, I'm not *ready* for that, OK?

SARA: *Are* you getting married?

ABBY: What do you mean, *are* we getting married?

SARA: The walls're here are thin, Abby. *Thin.* What'd you do last night? Heard you, what were you doing?

(Pause.)

ABBY: Exercises.

SARA: Uh-huh. You just best be careful, Abby, cause marriage is sacred. *(Sara begins setting the glasses on a shelf.)* I just think it's best you find some place, 'til the wedding.

ABBY: We'll see, yeah.

SARA: I mean it. I'm like real serious right now.

ABBY: OK.

(Pause. Abby picks up a wine glass, inspects it.)

ABBY: They're not even real glass.

(Sara grabs it from her.)

SARA: They're a thick durable PLASTIC so they break less. It's what Martha freakin' STEWART said to do so just lay off, you wanna tell her she's wrong?

ABBY: She *did* go to jail.

SARA: She's a good lady, everybody makes mistakes!

ABBY: It's just kinda white trash.

SARA: Excuse me, *What?*

ABBY: Nothin'.

(Sara begins putting the glasses away, pissed. She stops.)

SARA: If I'm so white trash then what're you?

ABBY: I am — I am *not* —

SARA: You coulda gone other places, Abby, you didn't have to stay here, you're always / bitchin' —

ABBY: I didn't have any *money* to go any places.

SARA: Where there's a will, there's a way!

ABBY: And what about you?

SARA: I never had any will! *(Pause.)* Hell, I don't care. You see this house? This house is fulla nice things.

ABBY: Rental.

SARA: Rent to OWN. You know how much money Ron makes a year? Sixty. Sixty THOUSAND. How much *you* make?

ABBY: How much do YOU make?

SARA: I make my FAMILY.

(She throws a wine glass. It bounces. They look at it. They don't know what to do so they laugh. Both are still hurt. Sara picks it up. Then puts it gently on the shelf. Sara stacks the glasses.)

SARA: My daughter's a little boy. She's not supposed to be like that, she's supposed to be like *me,* like mother like daughter.

(She sits at the table.)

SARA: What's that crap you drink, the zinfandel?

ABBY: White zinfandel, yeah.

SARA: I'm gonna have a glass a that.

ABBY: It's nine a.m.

SARA: Yeah, well, it's my kitchen and I do what I want.

OR
Liz Duffy Adams

Comic
Aphra, twenties
Nell, twenties

> *Actress Nell Gwynne has just met Aphra Behn, a poet and ex-spy who
> is soon to become the first professional female playwright. They are shar-
> ing a tobacco pipe in Aphra's rooms, sizing each other up and seducing
> each other — playfully at first, as playwrights and actors do. Nell grew
> up in her mother's brothel and sold oranges in the theater before be-
> coming the most successful actress of the new Restoration stage. She is
> young, unpretentious, outrageous, funny, and sensual. Slightly older
> than Nell, Aphra is another self-created woman, recently a Royalist spy,
> now aiming to break into the theater as a playwright. She is witty and
> charismatic, capable both of great warmth and of absolute steeliness of
> purpose. It's a love scene between two people, each of whom is usually
> the wittiest, sexiest, smartest person in the room — and who is thrilled
> to meet her match.*

NELL: Good weed.

APHRA: Isn't it?

NELL: Damned good weed. Where do you get it? I haven't been able to afford
it since they raised the tax.

APHRA: A friend is kind enough to get it for me.

NELL: A friend? Hmm, I wonder who is Aphra's friend. You're amazingly dis-
creet, no one knows. All right, I know, I'm a nosy bitch.

APHRA: Not at all.

NELL: Not at all but mind your damned business, Nell. Never mind. I'm still
so thrilled to meet you. I can't believe I had the nerve to come and bang
on your door unintroduced like this. Everyone says you're the next big
thing.

APHRA: Everyone?

NELL: That's the gossip. I swear, I thought I was climbing the stairs to fucking Olympus.

APHRA: Are you mad? I would have come to you weeks ago if I had dared, and thrown myself at the feet of the greatest actress of the new age! Your Florimell left me overcome with admiration.

NELL: Aw, don't be silly, I'm just an orange girl made good. You should have come backstage.

APHRA: Next time.

NELL: I'm not interrupting your work, am I?

APHRA: No, no, do forgive me the rudeness, but I've been promised an introduction to Lady Davenant of the Duke's Company and I need something new to show her; anyway I can write and chat at the same time.

NELL: That's a neat trick.

APHRA: O, I had to learn how. This is the first time in my life I've had a room of my own.

NELL: No family left, then?

APHRA: Finally managed to shrug them off; they're in the country.

NELL: Wasn't there a husband? A Dutchman?

APHRA: Plague.

NELL: Sorry.

APHRA: Don't be. What about you?

NELL: I'm on my own now; my last keeper had monstrous bad luck at gambling and had to retrench, but another one will come along soon. It's lucky that the aristos are all theater mad, isn't it? I suppose yours is someone very grand indeed, to get such good tobacco.

APHRA: Not at all.

NELL: Not at all! Christ, you've got good manners, you must think I'm a wretched guttersnipe.

(Aphra stops writing and looks at her.)

APHRA: I think you're absolute heaven.

NELL: O. That's nice.

Are you writing a part for me? No, I know, I'm with King's and my son-of-a-bitch producer would never let me out of my contract to play with the rivals.

APHRA: It's a shame. I do have a part for you, you'd be perfect in it. A beautiful Amazon warrior who falls madly in love with her enemy and is utterly undone.

NELL: O, you're killing me, I'd die to play that! We own all the old revival rights you know, all I get to play are the goddamned classics, where Dukes gets all the new plays. It's so unfair. A breeches part, I suppose?

APHRA: Yes, until the end when she succumbs to love and changes to women's clothes.

NELL: Yeah, see? So right for me. They love me in the breeches parts, so they can look at my legs.

APHRA: I don't blame them.

NELL: Yes, they're nice, aren't they? On the way over here a man really took me for a rent boy; I had to run away! Wouldn't he have been disappointed!

APHRA: Not necessarily. Might have swung both ways.

NELL: Is that what your friend is like?

APHRA: I think that's what most people are like, if they only knew it.

NELL: I don't know. I grew up in a brothel and I can tell you, some people are astonishingly particular about what they like; only one very specific thing will rouse 'em and nothing else will do. We had one regular fella who would have his favorite girl take off her stockings and wriggle her big toe into his — but maybe I'd better wait until I know you better. Am I shocking you?

APHRA: I didn't grow up in a brothel, but I hope nothing in that realm can shock me. Nature endowed us with a glorious gift for pleasure and nothing is more natural than to take all honest advantage of it.

NELL: And by honest you mean?

APHRA: Willing. The only sensual sin is to take what isn't freely given. If I am lucky enough to attract the true affection of a lovely man or woman, and if together we can increase the sum total of happiness in the world for even an hour, I consider that an act of virtue, not vice.

NELL: You are persuasive. I can't think how to argue with that, even if I wanted to.

APHRA: But you don't want to?

NELL: I don't.

APHRA: Shall I read you a bit from the play?

NELL: Yes, please.

APHRA: "Even now I was in love with mere report, with words, with empty noise; and now that flame, like to the breath that blew it, is vanished into air, and in its room an object quite unknown, unfamed, unheard of, informs my soul; how easily 'tis conquered!"

NELL: Did you just write that, while I was here? Am I the object that informs your soul?

APHRA: Mm hm.

(Aphra kisses her.)

NELL: This is strange.

APHRA: Not so strange, is it?

NELL: Well, no. Just sudden.

APHRA: Sudden love is truest, undisguised.

NELL: And she who sudden loves will take the prize.

APHRA: Nice.

NELL: Thanks. Sudden love steals sweet throughout my veins.

APHRA: And steals away what little wit remains.

NELL: Ha bloody ha. Your turn.

APHRA: By Cupid's sudden arrow I've been hit.

NELL: And suddenly your love is all I — shit.

APHRA: What?

NELL: Sorry, it wasn't going to rhyme!

APHRA: Idiot!

NELL: Critic!

(Another kiss.)

NELL: Who kisses better, me or your keeper?

APHRA: You bring him up so much, are you already jealous?

NELL: O, never jealous. He's just a man, I suppose. Where would any of us be without men to pay the rent?

APHRA: We can earn our own, I suppose?

NELL: Are you joking? I have to spend all my earnings on clothes and carriages, just to keep my reputation up.

APHRA: You could marry?

NELL: The fatherless daughter of a whorehouse keeper? Who do you think I could find to marry?

APHRA: I shudder to think.

NELL: Anyway, what's the difference, except you're selling yourself to just one man. No way around it, to be a woman is to be a whore and if God doesn't like it why did he make it that way? Though come to think of it, men are whores too.

APHRA: What, the men too?

NELL: That's right, every one of them, flirting and pandering and cocksucking their way all the way up the ladder! Any man that isn't a cocksucking trimming whore is probably dead; no way else to survive these slippery times. You laugh, but it's true, you know it is. Name me a man or woman in the kingdom can't be named whore.

APHRA: Well, but what about the king? Is he a cocksucking whore?

NELL: No, worse, a teasing whore! With one hand he tickles the balls of the Parliament while with the other he keeps his cousin Louis well fluffed, all to keep the money coming in. He dirty talks the Catholics until they're hard and hopeful, then turns around and jilts them when his ministers hold up a sack of cash. It's true! I don't blame him, I adore him — where would I be without him to reopen the theaters and set the fashion? But just between us, let's call a spade a goddamned shovel.

APHRA: O, my God, I love you, foul mouth and all.

NELL: Is it so foul?

APHRA: It's delicious . . . But I have to come to the king's defense. He wants to help the Catholics, he really believes in religious toleration —

NELL: But he needs money for the war, so his hands are tied, I know, I know. But don't let's talk about war and politics; it's such a bore and you must have had enough of all that in your previous career.

APHRA: My previous career?

NELL: Don't go all mumchance, everyone knows you were a spy.

APHRA: Everyone knows . . . ?

NELL: There are no secrets in the theater, it's much too small a world and all anyone does is gossip. Anyway, your mask is off with me now, isn't it?

APHRA: All right, it's true. And yes, I've had enough of it. It's a nasty little world of lies, subterfuge, backstabbing, and betrayal.

NELL: Wait, are we talking about spying or the theater?

APHRA: A man I was fond of was killed, not long after he was seen with me in Antwerp.

NELL: Was he a spy too?

APHRA: A double agent.

NELL: And you blame yourself for his death? I doubt it was your fault.

APHRA: You don't know anything about it.

NELL: I have some idea of what the life of a double agent must be like. Doubles your chances of someone wanting to slit your throat. Sorry; O, sorry, I'm a tactless cow.

APHRA: No, you're right, but it's an ugly world, isn't it. Don't you wish we could go far far away, back to a simpler time?

NELL: Was there ever a simple time since there were people in the world?

APHRA: There was, long ago.

> Before the wars of ministers and kings
> Before the need to struggle for our bread
> Before all strivings base and harsh there was
> A golden age of happiness sublime
> Where lovely nymphs — like you with fewer clothes —
> In fragrant groves lay hidden from the sun
> Which dappled through the leaves to gild their days

While night time 'neath the pearly moon there played
The gentle shepherdesses and their swains
Living all for music, poetry, love
All pleasures sweetly innocent enjoyed
Tumbling soft together, of all kinds
Before the grim unnatural rule of law
Of gods and men, O sweet Arcadia!
Pure freedom was the natural state of man
And woman, human spirit sanctified
In harmony with all the natural world
Unfettered, unrepressed, and unashamed
A happier better time could not be named.

NELL: Sounds fucking fabulous. And guess what — it sounds like right now. It's a new golden age, babe.

APHRA: Maybe it will be.

NELL: It is. The puritans had their day, now it's our turn. Peace, love, and happiness.

APHRA: Except for the war.

NELL: The war can't last forever.

APHRA: Maybe you're right.

NELL: Maybe nothing! Don't be such a nostalgia queen. Look around. We can love who we want, girls or boys; we can wear any clothes we want —

APHRA: Girl's or boy's.

NELL: Yeah! The world has changed. A woman can be an actress, a playwright, a poet, a libertine, a spy. A nobody like me is the it-girl everyone loves; you can shed your murky past to become the toast of the theater; every day and night is a party and a happening and a grand fucking festival of art and love. We are lucky to be alive right now. This is our utopia, and it's never going to end.

APHRA: How lovely it would be to believe that.

NELL: O, just chose to believe it, that's what I do. Tune in and turn on, just like this.

(Another kiss.)

APHRA: You have a genius for living in the moment. I believe you could make the saddest man in the world smile.

NELL: I certainly could, and I would, if he could pay my landlord. I'll have to choose someone soon but I can't make up my mind; plenty of rich admirers and each one as dull as a rainy day. Money's not enough, I have to have wit, don't you?

APHRA: Nell, I think I'm having a brilliant idea.

NELL: Are you?

APHRA: If I can get this play produced I'm sure it will be a success.

NELL: I like your confidence.

APHRA: Well, to be honest I swing back and forth between confidence and knowing for a fact that it will be the biggest bomb the London theater has ever seen and I'll be hounded by the shame into my grave. But let's assume it's a hit.

NELL: Yes, let's.

APHRA: Then I'll be able to keep myself. And I think you'd love my friend.

NELL: Thanks very much, but I don't need anyone's castoffs.

APHRA: O, you'd want this one.

NELL: Would I?

APHRA: Trust me.

NELL: Well, but wouldn't it cost you a pang, to pass him on to me?

APHRA: I'm never jealous. Possessive love is a sort of slavery, I abhor it. I love freely and I don't allow anyone to own me; how could I justify keeping anyone I love in chains? I love you both; if you loved each other my happiness would be multiplied, not diminished. Only still love me too; don't leave me; then I would believe in your new golden age, and we would all live there together.

NELL: Now I see why you haven't remarried. You're far too romantic.

APHRA: Yes. Though to be honest it's not pure altruism on my part. I can't make him happy and he'll soon find someone else anyway.

NELL: Who is he that a goddess like you can't make him happy? Fuck 'im, he's too fussy for me.

APHRA: No, it's fair enough. I won't . . . I don't care to . . . Well, to be blunt, I don't let him fuck me. We exchange every other pleasure but that.

NELL: Why not?

APHRA: For one thing, I don't want to get knocked up.

NELL: O, if that's all, there are ways.

APHRA: I know, and none of them can be counted on. Anyway, if we're really letting our hair down, I've never really cared that much about that part; it's all the rest that does it for me.

NELL: I love it, I could do it for hours. Did you see my Cleopatra last season? "O happy horse, to bear the weight of Antony!" I love that line, I know just what she means.

OUR HOUSE
Theresa Rebeck

Seriocomic
Alice, twenties to thirties
Merv, twenties to thirties

> *Alice and Merv live with two other people in a house. Alice is the house*
> *treasurer, and she is very concerned that Merv is not paying his share.*
> *Here, she confronts him about it.*

ALICE: Good evening, Merv.

MERV: Alice hi, how are you today? Wow check her out. How much work has
she had done? Nobody looks like that. Barbie looks like that. Malibu
nose-job Barbie.

   I mean I hate it when gorgeous women cut their hair like that, it's
like I'm so beautiful I can cut it all off and look I'm still great looking,
it's so aggressive. It's like look at me! Look at my bone structure! She
probably hasn't had plastic surgery, I take it back. But she is so skinny, I
don't believe it for one second. She probably spends half her life in the
bathroom throwing up.

ALICE: OK these ramblings about Jennifer Ramirez are truly fascinating

MERV: They're not ramblings. It's my personal exegesis about the fetishization
of the female form. I mean it's not like I'm, but it is, what is she doing
on *Our House*? She's Miss Morning News! Except it's not the real news
anymore it's hi, let's talk about really stupid shit and pretend that you're
like on a date with Jennifer Ramirez kind of news. Fucking retard. Wow
is she pretty. I love this show. I just love it. It's so spectacularly trashy.
(Alice mutes the television.)

ALICE: Great. Look, we have to have a house meeting this weekend to talk
about bills and next year's lease.

MERV: Well, that's super, Alice. I'll really be looking forward to that.
(He reaches for the clicker; she takes it with her, casual, a couple steps away.)

ALICE: We're going to have to balance the books for the fiscal year, so everyone is going to have to rectify their house account. Is that going to be a
problem for you?

MERV: It depends on what exactly you mean by "rectify your house account," Alice. To my unpracticed ear it sounds a little like you're trolling for sexual favors. But I have a feeling that's not what you think you're doing.

ALICE: No, the point I'm trying to make is a tad more financial. Here's what you owe.

(She hands him a sheet of paper.)

MERV: What I "owe"?

ALICE: What you owe, three months rent on the year, and there's what you owe on the groceries and the house expenses.

MERV: And what's this?

ALICE: Let's see what does it say? "Interest." That's the interest that you owe to the rest of us for carrying your debt for part of the year.

MERV: You expect me to pay interest. To you.

ALICE: I expect you to pay forty-two hundred and seven dollars and sixty-three cents, to the house account, on Saturday. If you can't pay that, we're going to have a discussion about whether or not you should be here, next year.

MERV: You're kicking me out! What the fuck, you think you're kicking me out of my own house?

ALICE: I'm not kicking you out, Merv —

MERV: You flicking bitch!

ALICE: Oh that's great —

MERV: You fucking think you're going to kick me out of my own house —

ALICE: I am just telling you the facts! If you are not able to keep up with your share of the house expenses you need to find a place you can afford!

MERV: This is my house, this isn't your house!

ALICE: See you Saturday. You might want to put on some fucking pants.

(He turns, dismissing her, and clicks on the television set.)

PARASITE DRAG
Mark Roberts

More information on this author may be found on the "Meet the Authors" web page at www.smithandkraus.com.

Seriocomic
Joellen Brown, midthirties to forties
Susie Brown, midthirties to forties

Joellen and Susie are left alone while husbands Ronnie and Gene are out making funeral arrangements for their sister, who has just died of AIDS. The two women begin to bond over the death of their sister-in-law, each one revealing truths not only about the family they married into but about themselves.

(Joellen sits at the kitchen table, still in her bathrobe. She's sipping coffee. After a beat, she crosses to the kitchen counter with her cup. She refills it. Susie enters.)

SUSIE: *(Yawning.)* Morning.

JOELLEN:. Good morning.

SUSIE: I figured I'd be the only one up this early.

JOELLEN: How'd you sleep?

SUSIE: Like a fat dog on a warm rug.

JOELLEN: *(Smiling.)* Coffee?

SUSIE: Thank you. *(Susie crosses to the table and sits.)* How'd *you* sleep?

JOELLEN: I didn't . . . really.

SUSIE: Didn't sleep at all?

JOELLEN: I have real bad insomnia. *(Joellen crosses to her with a cup of coffee. She sets it in front of her and sits.)* I can grab maybe a half hour at a time, if I'm lucky. Then my mind just screams itself awake.

SUSIE: Must have a lot going on in there.

JOELLEN: I guess. I just stare at the ceiling, until the alarm goes off.

SUSIE: See now, they say you should get up and do something, instead of just laying there.

JOELLEN: Really?

SUSIE: Busy yourself, is what they say. I read it . . . an article someplace. This woman had terrible insomnia, and she would get up and do stuff. Instead of just laying there. At first she would clean, or do a crossword puzzle. Still couldn't sleep. Then, she started baking.

JOELLEN: Baking?

SUSIE: Yeah. Bread, cookies. She'd just bake all night long.

JOELLEN: And that helped her sleep?

SUSIE: No. But, she ended up opening a bed and breakfast and marketing her own line of breads and muffins. I think she even wrote a cookbook. *(Beat.)* You know when I think about it, the point of that article was not curing insomnia, but how to start your own small business. *(Beat.)* Do you like to bake?

JOELLEN: No.

SUSIE: Well, I wish I had more to offer on the subject. But I guess the gist of it is "don't just lay there." *(Pause. They sip their coffee.)* Where the boys at this early?

JOELLEN: Their sister passed away last night.

SUSIE: *(Sighing.)* Oh, no.

JOELLEN: Yeah.

SUSIE: When?

JOELLEN: Got the call around two.

SUSIE: Oh, good Lord.

JOELLEN: Nurse walked in to check on her, and . . . she was gone, poor thing.

SUSIE: I wish Ronnie would have woke me. Where they at now?

JOELLEN: Funeral home.

SUSIE: Was he real upset? I mean, I'm sure he was upset, but —

JOELLEN: He seemed OK.

SUSIE: He takes this stuff so hard. Oh my. How old was she, anyway?

JOELLEN: Would have been forty-eight next month.

SUSIE: That's so young.

JOELLEN: With the drugs and everything, looked like she was twice that age.

SUSIE: There's a price to pay for everything.

JOELLEN: It was hard to watch, I'll tell you that. She just withered away.

SUSIE: What a shame.

JOELLEN: She was such a beautiful little girl, too.

SUSIE: Really?

JOELLEN: Gorgeous little thing.

SUSIE: You don't have any pictures, do you?

JOELLEN: Most of it's packed away in the garage, but . . . let me see.

(Joellen crosses to a small hutch in the living room and pulls out two photo albums.)

SUSIE: I guess in a way this is a blessing.

JOELLEN: I'm just glad it's over. I mean . . . well.

(Joellen crosses to the kitchen table with the albums and sits.)

SUSIE: You know, I have never seen one picture of Ronnie as a boy.

JOELLEN: Doesn't surprise me.

SUSIE: Not even a school photo.

JOELLEN: Ronnie has never been one to look back.

SUSIE: Well, he did own a couple of cars he speaks pretty fondly of. But, that's about it.

(Joellen points to a picture.)

JOELLEN: That's her. That's Nadine.

SUSIE: What a little sweetheart.

JOELLEN: She must have been around four or five there.

SUSIE: Those blue eyes. Oh my gosh.

JOELLEN: Yeah, she was something else.

SUSIE: What a shame. *(Pause.)*

JOELLEN: *(Pointing to the album.)* Recognize him?

SUSIE: *(Looking.)* You're kidding me?

JOELLEN: None other.

SUSIE: He looks so weird with hair.

JOELLEN: Already starting to recede.

SUSIE: Oh, my gosh. *(Beat.)* He played football?

JOELLEN: You really don't know any of this stuff?

SUSIE: He won't talk about anything growing up.

JOELLEN: Nothing?

SUSIE: Says it's history, none of it amounts to anything.

JOELLEN: One of the best football players that school ever had. Very athletic.

SUSIE: You're kidding me. I gotta stick a bomb up his butt to get him to take out the garbage.

JOELLEN: He'd run up and down that field, with his long hair spilling out of his helmet.

SUSIE: And so, you knew him in school?

JOELLEN: Sure did.

SUSIE: How was he . . . I mean, what kind of a boy was he?

JOELLEN: *(Sighing.)* Well, he marched to his own drummer, that's for sure.

SUSIE: Sounds about right. Was he popular, or . . . ?

JOELLEN: He was. Friendly with everybody. You'd see him in the parking lot talking to some boy nobody else would give the time of day to.

SUSIE: He's good that way. There's a retarded kid in our apartment complex and Ronnie bought him a wiffle ball bat.

JOELLEN: He always took people at face value. Treated everybody the same.

SUSIE: He's still like that. Although, I will say he gets a little impatient with waitresses, or anybody that's handling his food.

JOELLEN: When I moved here, I was fifteen, had no friends. Tried to blend into the background as much as I could. I remember one day, some boys were teasing me in the hallway. I can't even remember about what. But, Ronnie walked up, kind of sized up the situation, and just started talking to me. Carrying on a real conversation with me. Didn't make a big deal out of it. Those other boys quietly slumped away. And then every day after that, he'd make a point of stopping by my locker and checking in on me. It got me through that first year. And the thing I . . . loved the most about him was he never acted like he didn't know you. If he was hanging out with a bunch of his friends and you walked by, he said "hello" and was real friendly. Tried to include you. He seemed to have a sort of a distance from everything. Like he was standing apart from all of it. You know what I mean?

SUSIE: Yes, I do.

JOELLEN: He was quite a young man.

SUSIE: Did you have a crush on him? *(Pause.)*

JOELLEN: Still do.

(Susie smiles. Pause. Their eyes meet. Susie stops smiling.)

JOELLEN: How'd the two of you meet?

SUSIE: He used to work at this building right next to the "Curves," and I'd see him outside smoking all the time. Holding court with the other nicotine fiends. Always holding court. You could tell he was funny, the other people were always laughing at everything he was saying. And I like funny men. Don't need rich or a big you-know-what. Just . . . have to be funny. Anyway, I got up the nerve to wander over there. And we got to talking . . . and eventually, I just kind of fell . . . in love with him.

JOELLEN: Good for you.

SUSIE: Well, he is a handful, I will say that.

JOELLEN: Tell me something I don't know.

SUSIE: Took a while to get him to settle down. I mean, as much as he'll ever settle down. But, I know he loves me, and he's faithful. For the most part.

(Joellen looks at her.)

SUSIE: He's a man, what are you gonna do? They'll wander off the road just to see how muddy their shoes get.

JOELLEN: You're OK with that?

SUSIE: It don't mean nothing. Just sex. Just don't bring anything home that I can catch. Half the time it's just boredom on his part, anyway.

JOELLEN: You don't get jealous?

SUSIE: What's the point? I figure it's just some lonely old skank who'd mess with a married man. And to him it's not much more than jerking off. Pardon my language.

(Joellen smiles weakly.)

SUSIE: Is Gene faithful?

JOELLEN: I would assume. Who knows. You can't ever really know. Truthfully, I don't think he's interested in it one way or the other.

SUSIE: He's not interested in it at all?

(Pause. Joellen looks at her.)

SUSIE: Sorry. Too personal.

JOELLEN: No, it's fine.

SUSIE: I'm too nosy.

JOELLEN: No, no. Midwesterners like to play it close to the vest, is all.

SUSIE: I'm from the South. We'll dump it in your lap, whether you want it or not.

(They smile. Pause.)

JOELLEN: He's never been an overly affectionate man.

SUSIE: Not even when you were first dating?

JOELLEN: He was real sweet and attentive, but he just never seemed to care about . . . the other. One night I ended up throwing myself at him. He did his best. But, it was very awkward.

SUSIE: Did it get better?

JOELLEN: Not really. We figured out a way to get through it and tell ourselves it was OK. But, it wasn't. After a while we stopped trying altogether. Just seemed better to avoid the discomfort.

SUSIE: *(Tentatively.)* How long has it been? *(Pause.)*

JOELLEN: Eight years.

SUSIE: Holy fuck. *(Beat.)* Sorry.

(Joellen looks at her. They laugh.)

SUSIE: Sorry.

JOELLEN: It's all right.

SUSIE: Man, oh man. I go longer than two weeks, I start rubbing my butt on doorknobs. *(They laugh.)*

JOELLEN: *(Pointing at a photo.)* That's Gene.

SUSIE: How old was he there?

JOELLEN: Must've been around thirteen. Right around the time their mama died.

SUSIE: Did you know her at all?

JOELLEN: Gene and I started dating after she passed away. I've seen pictures of her. Beautiful woman.

SUSIE: How'd she die?

JOELLEN: You don't know any of this?

(Susie shakes her head. Pause.)

JOELLEN: Their mama killed herself. *(Pause.)*

SUSIE: How?

JOELLEN: She drove out to Willard Airport, parked her car in the lot, walked out to a field near the runway, drank two cans of Miller Hi-Life, laid down and shot herself in the mouth. Just as an airplane passed over head.

SUSIE: Jesus Christ.

JOELLEN: Women generally don't kill themselves in such a violent fashion. Usually take pills or slash their wrists.

SUSIE: I guess when you're done, you're done. *(Pause. Pointing to a picture.)* Is that their dad?

JOELLEN: That's Carl.

SUSIE: Ronnie won't talk about his daddy, except in the most hateful terms.

JOELLEN: Well, Carl . . . was not a nice person.

SUSIE: One of the only things I've heard was the two of them getting in a fight in the front yard . . .

JOELLEN: I've heard that story.

SUSIE: What was your version?

JOELLEN: Apparently, Ronnie used the F-word on Carl . . .

SUSIE: He loves that word.

JOELLEN: Well, his daddy didn't. And after Ronnie said it to him, Carl picked him up and threw him against the wall. Ronnie came back at him with a glass ashtray and broke it across his head. They spilled out into the front yard with it. Neighbors standing on their porches watching. Police finally came and broke it up. And Ronnie walked away from the house that day and never came back. Not even for his dad's funeral.

SUSIE: Ronnie told me his daddy said he never wanted to lay eyes on him again.

JOELLEN: In one family you can get five different versions of the same story. And every person was affected by it in five different ways.

SUSIE: I guess my family is kind of odd.

JOELLEN: How so?

SUSIE: We all just love and accept one another.

JOELLEN: *(Smiling.)* Funny that's considered odd these days.

SUSIE: Not to say we don't fuss, but nothing like Ronnie's side. We enjoy each other too much. My daddy was very big on family. And the rest of us are, too. I remember the first time I took Ronnie to meet them, he was all nervous in the car. Fretting and snappin' at me. And then whens we got there, I think we'd only been there about twenty minutes, he was laughing and cuttin' up. On the drive home, he said, "Wow, your family really seems to like each other." It was such a foreign concept to him.

JOELLEN: You think whatever you grew up with is what's normal. Then when you get a chance to see other families, you realize how fucked up yours is.

SUSIE: *(Laughing.)* Now we got you saying it.

JOELLEN: I've said it before.

(They both smile. Joellen stops. Her face remorseful. They look through the album.)

SUSIE: Is that Nadine?

JOELLEN: She must've been a teenager there.

SUSIE: What's she frowning about, I wonder?

JOELLEN: Hard to tell.

SUSIE: So sad.

JOELLEN: You know, Gene says God has a plan for all of us. Do you believe that?

SUSIE: I think things just happen.

JOELLEN: That's what I think. I mean, assuming there is a God, assuming He has a plan, why is He coddling some of us and letting the rest of us run in traffic?

SUSIE: You'd think he wouldn't play favorites.

JOELLEN: Doesn't seem very "God-like."

SUSIE: I'm very conflicted when it comes to the Lord. I was raised Baptist, and that's enough to sour you on Him for a lifetime. I mean, the Bible has a lot of good things to say, lot of valuable lessons. But, once it gets filtered through all the assholes "spreading His word," it becomes convoluted and highly suspect, in my opinion. But, I do believe the original intent was good.

JOELLEN: It's just all so fear-based. Fear and punishment. You know, when I got in trouble as a kid, my mom used to say, "You're gonna see the devil at the foot of your bed tonight."

SUSIE: Really?

JOELLEN: Uh-huh.

SUSIE: What a horrible thing to tell a child.

JOELLEN: I'd just lay there all night, staring at the foot of my bed. Terrified, that any minute, the devil was gonna pop his head up, grab me, and take me down to hell with him.

SUSIE: Was your mom crazy?

JOELLEN: Methodist.

SUSIE: Well.

JOELLEN: When I got older I forgot all about her saying that. It would flash through my head once in a while, but I never dwelled on it. Then, about a month ago, I came home from the hospital, laid down just to rest my eyes. At one point I was half awake, half asleep. I looked down at the foot of the bed, and there he was.

SUSIE: The devil?

JOELLEN: Uh-huh.

SUSIE: Like you dreamed it, or . . . ?

JOELLEN: I don't know. I honestly don't.

SUSIE: That gives me the chills.

JOELLEN: He wasn't scary, like I thought he'd look as a kid. He was old and wrinkled. And the thing I remember the most was his smile. It was a smile that saw right through me. As if to say "You're not fooling anybody."

SUSIE: Fooling anybody about what?

JOELLEN: The whole time I was sitting with Nadine in the hospital, I was praying she would die.

SUSIE: 'Cause she was suffering and all.

JOELLEN: No. I mean, that was part of it. *(Pause.)*

SUSIE: I don't understand. *(Pause.)*

JOELLEN: I'm leaving my husband.

SUSIE: Really? *(Pause.)*

JOELLEN: When his sister got sick, I put it off.

SUSIE: Does he know?

JOELLEN: No. Didn't seem right to leave him now with such a full plate. But I told myself that as soon as she passed, I'd be gone. So, I'd sit next to that poor girl and pray that God would take her. Take her, so her suffering would end. But, it wasn't really her suffering I wanted to end.

SUSIE: It was yours.

JOELLEN: Mine. *(Pause.)*

SUSIE: Well, I guess your prayers got answered. *(Pause.)*

JOELLEN: Do you think I'm a bad person?

SUSIE: It's not up to me to judge you one way or the other. *(Beat.)* But, it might explain why you can't sleep at night.

(Lights slowly fade.)

ROSALEE WAS HERE
Maura Campbell

More information on this author may be found on the "Meet the Authors" web page at www.smithandkraus.com.

Dramatic
Rosalee, fourteen
Molly, twenties to thirties

> *Rosalee, an eighth-grade girl, has just returned from juvenile detention and is secluded with her teacher's aide, Molly, in a private classroom. She tries to pick up her life at school but is hampered by overmedication and insecurity. Molly tries various ways to reach the mercurial girl but is, for the most part, out of her depth.*

ROOM 313

MOLLY: How was your time away?

ROSALEE: I don't want to talk about it.

MOLLY: OK. Do you want to go to class?

ROSALEE: Nooo . . . I just want to sleep. It's this medication. I'm like a zombie.

MOLLY: What are you taking?

ROSALEE: Who knows — like four different pills — they think I might be preschizophrenic.

MOLLY: What makes them think that?

ROSALEE: Because I told them that God talks to me. He won't do it anymore.

MOLLY: Who won't?

ROSALEE: God. It's the pills. They're anti-God pills. Here.
(She hands Molly a paper.)

MOLLY: Wow, Rose, this is really . . . real.

ROSALEE: I made most of it up.

MOLLY: I think if you get rid of the first paragraph, just go right into the description of the place . . . why is it so cold?

ROSALEE: They do that to keep you alert. Fifty-eight degrees. I just made up the part about the vomit. There wasn't really a pile of it in the cell with me. But there could have been. The other girl they brought in was drunk. Are you still reading that Shakespeare book?

MOLLY: It's for a class. I have to read two of his plays and all of his sonnets.

ROSALEE: What's a sonnet?

MOLLY: A poem with three quatrains and a rhyming couplet written in iambic pentameter.

ROSALEE: *(Interrupting.)* OK, more than I wanted to know.

MOLLY: In my presentation I have to memorize one.

ROSALEE: Good luck!

MOLLY: It's not until the middle of December. I'll start, oh, the middle of December. Stay up all one night, drink a lot of coffee.

ROSALEE: Like I said, it would help if he wrote in English.

MOLLY: I'm thinking of memorizing this one. Number seventeen.

ROSALEE: *(Reads.)* Who will believe my verse in time to come,
If it were fill'd with your most high deserts?
High deserts?

MOLLY: It's means gifts. Like beauty. Kindness. Intelligence.

ROSALEE: Oh.
Who will believe my verse in time to come,
If it were fill'd with your most high deserts?
Though yet heaven knows it is but as a tomb
Which hides your life, and shows not half your parts.
If I could write the beauty of your eyes,
And in fresh numbers number all your graces,
The age to come would say 'This poet lies;
Such heavenly touches ne'er touch'd earthly faces.'
So should my papers, yellow'd with their age,
Be scorn'd, like old men of less truth than tongue,
And your true rights be term'd a poet's rage.
And stretched metre of an antique song:
But were some child of yours alive that time,
You should live twice, in it, and in my rhyme.
That's beautiful.

MOLLY: Do you know what it means?

ROSALEE: No. But some things are just beautiful without thinking about them. Can we find Ethan now? I have to give him a letter. He asked me to go to the dance and if I don't tell him yes he'll ask someone else. Please?

MOLLY: Rose, we don't even know where —

ROSALEE: I know where he is, he's in science. We'll just go to the door and ask for him and give him the note. I don't have phone privileges at home so I can't call him. Please?

MOLLY: How about you give me the note —

ROSALEE: No! You won't do it!

MOLLY: I will. I promise —

ROSALEE: You're a liar! You always lie!

MOLLY: I'm not lying, if you'll just give me a chance —

ROSALEE: No! You're a big fat liar!

MOLLY: OK! OK! It's OK! We'll give him the note! Please — come out of there — come here. I'm sorry. I know it's really important to you. Let's go do it. OK? Come on.

ROSALEE: We really will?

MOLLY: We really will.

ROSALEE: This better not be a trick.

MOLLY: No tricks.

ROSALEE: He's the most popular boy in the whole school.

MOLLY: I know who he is. He's really . . . cute.

ROSALEE: God, it's gross when you say it.

MOLLY: Have you got the letter?

ROSALEE: Just sit over there! . . . OK. All done. But when he comes to the door, you have to stand away and act like you're doing something else.

MOLLY: Rosalee —

ROSALEE: Just a little ways! God, you can still hear me, I just don't want you in my face! This is my boyfriend!

MOLLY: I'll stand away.

ROSALEE: Why are you all dressed up?

MOLLY: I have an interview. For a doctor. A doctor's appointment.

ROSALEE: What for?

MOLLY: Just female stuff.

ROSALEE: Are you pregnant?

MOLLY: No!

HALLWAY

MOLLY: *(Continued.)* This is the science room.

ROSALEE: I thought he was in science, I think he's in health.

(A bell rings. Rosalee becomes frightened.)

ROSALEE: You know what? I don't think he's even in school today. I think he's out sick. Duh! Now I remember he told me . . . he told me last week . . . he was going to call in sick today . . . because there was a test — I need to go to the nurse. I need Advil.

MOLLY: I have some Advil.

ROSALEE: I have to get it from the nurse! It's against the law for you to give it to me! We could both get arrested! This is a school! There are rules!

MOLLY: I'm sorry.

ROSALEE: Don't you know anything? Now I won't go to the dance. This was my last chance! Fuck it, I don't want to go to the dance anyway. Stupid kids getting dressed up.

MOLLY: What would you like to do right now that would make you feel better? Can you tell me?

ROSALEE: Drop dead maybe!

MOLLY: Hey, hey. It's all right. It's all going to be all right.

(Molly puts her arms around Rosalee and holds her a few moments. Rosalee starts to relax.)

MOLLY: Suppose we just breathe.

ROSALEE: I don't want to breathe.

MOLLY: Want to help me with my story?

ROSALEE: No. What story?

MOLLY: I'm writing a story about a girl named Mandy. She's thirteen and she really wants to get a part in the school play.

ROSALEE: What is it with you and plays?

MOLLY: The problem is that she stutters. I mean, her dream is to be an actress but she can't speak without effort.

ROSALEE: How does it start?

MOLLY: It starts with her in front of the class giving an oral presentation.

ROSALEE: Oh, God, that's the worst!

MOLLY: Of course there's this boy . . .

ROSALEE: Naturally . . .

MOLLY: Who she knows will get the part opposite her . . .

ROSALEE: Is he cute?

MOLLY: What do you think?

ROSALEE: Can't she just take a pill so she won't stutter?

MOLLY: Then there would be no story. She's got to overcome this obstacle.

ROSALEE: She's got to have a breakthrough!

SCAB

Sheila Callaghan

More information on this author may be found on the "Meet the Authors" web page at www.smithandkraus.com.

Dramatic
Anima, twenty-three
Christa, twenty-two

> *Anima and Christa are newly minted best friends and roommates who both hide devastating secrets from one another. Christa's secret: She slept with Anima's ex-boyfriend the previous evening. Anima's secret: She is falling in love with Christa. (Note: A backslash [/] indicates where the next line of dialogue overlaps the current one.)*

(Christa enters with a pastry box.)

ANIMA: Where'd you go?

CHRISTA: Hang-over pastries.

ANIMA: You are a superhero.

(Anima digs into the box.)

CHRISTA: It's so warm outside, I can't believe it's October, did you ever notice how all the palm trees bend toward the ocean, I was trying to figure out if they were stretching to get closer to the water or farther away from the mountains

ANIMA: No idea, did you get any Boston creams?

CHRISTA: They were out.

ANIMA: Those mother fuckers. How's your head?

CHRISTA: Fine. How's your hand?

ANIMA: Fine

CHRISTA: Let me see.

(Christa examines Anima's hand as Anima eats a donut.)

CHRISTA: Have you been picking at it

ANIMA: Yes

CHRISTA: Stop. It needs to scab.

ANIMA: I can't help it

(Christa disappears into the bathroom.)

ANIMA: Susan lost another leaf . . .

(Christa emerges with a Band-Aid and antiseptic, having not heard Anima. She begins cleaning Anima's wound.)

ANIMA: I read your paper yesterday.

CHRISTA: You did?

ANIMA: The whole thing.

CHRISTA: What did you think?

ANIMA: I loved it. I mean, my background in French history is not exactly comprehensive . . . but I was totally with it.

CHRISTA: Really?

ANIMA: Yeah. Like when Colette showed her tits on stage and they called her courageous. She's all bad-ass and brazen, like a DIVA. And it was pretty freaky to be inside your head like that. Freaky, freaky stuff.

CHRISTA: I'm so glad you liked it . . .

ANIMA: But it completely makes sense. Why you're interested in those women.

(A beat.)

CHRISTA: What do you mean?

ANIMA: You know. Neat, educated, middle class. By the book all the way. Dying to get the fuck out and do a little hardcore shake-and-bake. But sorta . . . you know. *(A beat.)* Anyway. Good reading. *(A beat.)*

CHRISTA: How are the donuts.

ANIMA: Yummy.

CHRISTA: And how are classes?

ANIMA: Also yummy.

(Christa looks up at Anima.)

ANIMA: What?

CHRISTA: You haven't been going.

ANIMA: Who told you

CHRISTA: A friend of yours.

ANIMA: WHO.

CHRISTA: A friend who was at the bar last night.

ANIMA: I have no friends.

CHRISTA: A classmate

ANIMA: Who who who?

CHRISTA: Tell me why you haven't been going to class first.

ANIMA: I haven't felt like it.

CHRISTA: Why not?

ANIMA: School makes me grouchy.

CHRISTA: Why don't you take a semester or two off?

ANIMA: For what? To remember why I'm supposed to be sad? I don't have to remember. It's my skin now.

CHRISTA: You can't just not go

ANIMA: One of my professors is this hundred-and-eighty-year-old Marxist evangelist who speaks extemporaneously for hours and makes grown men and women weep in class. Tears, I shit you not. But I never do. I try to look all enthralled but at the break I bolt from the room and burrow in the stairwell and scream into my sleeve.

CHRISTA: Maybe grad school isn't for you.

ANIMA: What else is there?

CHRISTA: You tell me.

ANIMA: If I knew that I wouldn't be here.

CHRISTA: What do you like to do?

ANIMA: What do I like to do . . . I like to act. I'm a really good actor. I did a lot of plays in college. Never got leads but I always kicked ass in the bit parts. And I fucking love theater. The body fluids and cigarette smoke and bad breath, the fucking, the drinking, the injured souls. I want to do nasty plays. The kind where you get nekkid on stage and everyone stares at your nipples.

CHRISTA: You're clearly not an academic.

ANIMA: Yeah, but it's free. I'm playing ball with my financial hardship here. Now who's my friend.

CHRISTA: It was Alan. He's worried about you.

(Anima is dead quiet. She pulls her bandaged hand from Christa's grasp.)

ANIMA: What else did he say?

CHRISTA: You haven't been returning his calls.

ANIMA: What else.

CHRISTA: I don't know.

(Anima grabs Christa's wrist.)

ANIMA: He told you things.

CHRISTA: You're hurting me.

(Anima lets go of Christa's wrist.)

ANIMA: Don't. Listen to me. DO NOT take his side on this.

CHRISTA: Side, what are you talking about, you were only seeing each other a month.

(Anima is quiet.)

CHRISTA: He's your friend and he cares about you /

ANIMA: I don't want to talk about it.

(A beat.)

CHRISTA: Fine.

(A beat. Anima walks over to the tapes. She begins playing with them.)

ANIMA: What's on these?

CHRISTA: My entire life since freshman year when I got my camcorder.

ANIMA: What are you saving them for?

CHRISTA: Nothing. Myself. Someday I'll make an epic montage of all my favorite moments and set it to James Taylor's "Smiling Face."

ANIMA: You are a supreme freak.

CHRISTA: I know.

ANIMA: Let's watch 'em . . .

CHRISTA: I can't, I've got a meeting.

ANIMA: On a Saturday.

CHRISTA: With my cohort.

ANIMA: Oh. OK. I'll just watch 'em while you're gone.

CHRISTA: You wouldn't.

ANIMA: What difference does it make, I don't know anybody in them.

CHRISTA: Look, we'll watch them when I get home, OK?

ANIMA: Goodie. Are you naked in any of them?

CHRISTA: Only the ones with your mom.

ANIMA: Score!

(Christa grabs her camcorder and her things to leave.)

CHRISTA: Is that one of the shirts we bought the other day?

CHRISTA: Yes.

ANIMA: I like it. Makes your boobs look all juicy. Like beefsteak tomatoes.

CHRISTA: Thanks.

ANIMA: Don't be mad at me.

CHRISTA: I'm not. I'm just late. I'll see you later.

(She kisses Anima and exits.)

THE SECRET LIFE OF SEAGULLS
Henry Meyerson

Seriocomic
Anne, midthirties
Sandy, midthirties

> *Good friends Anne and Sandy meet at a Florida beach to support each other as each is in the midst of separation from her spouse.*

SANDY: Just like that?

ANNE: Exactly. Isn't that strange?

SANDY: I've heard of these things happening.

ANNE: Really?

SANDY: Oh, sure. *(Pause.)* Well, come to think of it maybe not. Just got up and left, huh?

ANNE: Just got up and left.

SANDY: Without a word.

ANNE: No. Let me think. Ah. He said, "I'm going."

SANDY: "I'm going."

ANNE: That's what he said, Sandy, "I'm going."

SANDY: What did you think he meant?

ANNE: What do you mean?

SANDY: Well, did you think Don meant he'll be right back, or that he was going to the bathroom, or that he was, I don't know, leaving.

ANNE: Leaving as in . . . ?

SANDY: Leaving leaving.

ANNE: I didn't give it much thought at the time. I guess I figured he'd be right back. That he had to tinkle or something. No reason to think otherwise.

SANDY: What were you guys doing?

ANNE: Just sitting here chatting about the beach, the sky, the water and about our honeymoon. I thought it was a nice romantic time. Then he said "I'm going" and then he left.

SANDY: A week ago.

ANNE: Tomorrow will be a week. Strange, don't you think?

SANDY: That Don left or that you waited a week to call anyone?

ANNE: That he left.

SANDY: But why did you wait so long to call?

ANNE: I told you. I thought he was coming back.

SANDY: Annie, it's been a week.

ANNE: Tomorrow.

SANDY: What have you been doing for the past week in this hotel alone?

ANNE: Waiting. It is nice here, isn't it?

SANDY: So restful.

ANNE: Quiet.

SANDY: Except for the seagulls.

ANNE: What's wrong with the seagulls.

SANDY: All that squawking. *(Makes squawking sound.)* Sounds eerie at night. *(Makes squawking sound.)*

ANNE: For some reason I find that sound reassuring. *(Pause.)*

SANDY: I left him.

ANNE: Who?

SANDY: Jim.

ANNE: I assumed that when you got off the plane without him.

SANDY: You knew I left Jim?

ANNE: He's not here, is he? So, yeah, I figured you left him when you came down here.

SANDY: I don't mean I just left him. I left left him.

ANNE: Left left?

SANDY: As in adios, Jimmy, baby.

ANNE: Why?

SANDY: Golf. Golf, golf, golf. Endless playing, then endlessly talking about it.

ANNE: Is that a good enough reason to leave your husband?

SANDY: It was for me, kiddo.

ANNE: What did he say?

SANDY: I told you. He was talking about golf.

ANNE: I mean when you told him you were leaving.

SANDY: Since I didn't tell him I was leaving, not much he could have said.

ANNE: You just up and left?

SANDY: Between the seventh and eighth holes.

ANNE: Just like Don. Not a word, up and left.

SANDY: Except no seagulls.

ANNE: Do you think Jim knows you've gone away?

SANDY: Since I didn't tell him, he probably hasn't even noticed.

ANNE: Oh, he must have noticed. After a while he'd notice.

SANDY: Took you a week. Don goes for a pee, doesn't come back for a week and you figure he was going for the world record for taking the longest leak in history.

ANNE: I knew he was gone, Sandy. I just didn't realize he had gone gone. There's a difference. I asked if you think Jim noticed you had gone or had gone gone.

SANDY: A distinction without a difference.

ANNE: I don't know what that means.

SANDY: It means Jim just doesn't give a shit either way.

ANNE: Oh, I don't believe . . .

SANDY: It all became perfectly clear to me on the seventh hole.

ANNE: What did?

SANDY: He was putting out or digging a divot or whatever and I just realized he would rather be doing that than be with me.

ANNE: Excuse me, Sandy, but a lot of woman are golf widows.

SANDY: And a lot of women are schmucks, Anne. Ten years of trailing him around the country, course by course, hole by hole, divot by divot. Enough. Enough "Where'd the fucking ball go?" Enough watching him throw the clubs into the pond. And more than enough, thank you, of "birdy wordy."

ANNE: What?

SANDY: He says that sometimes when he's playing and it seems to make him very happy.

ANNE: *(Puzzled.)* Birdy wordy. What do you think it means?

SANDY: Am I attractive?

ANNE: Well . . .

SANDY: Am I attractive!

ANNE: Yes.

SANDY: Would men find me appealing?

ANNE: Sure.

SANDY: Do I have a right to determine my future?

ANNE: Of course.

SANDY: Then no more birdy wordies, Anne. Never again.

ANNE: Can't say I blame you.

SANDY: Blame me? I should be applauded for putting up with him for so long. I was just up to here *(Touches her throat.)* with him. Fed up.

ANNE: Do you think that's why Don walked out?

SANDY: Birdy wordies?

ANNE: Being fed up with me.

No olde thyme glamour
Lord knows we all hoped that a novel of crystalline detail,
An old-fashioned novel of "biting satire and dystopian leanings"
A novel that both pushed the form forward and yet referred back in time
To the Classics
To the Western Canon
A novel like that might somehow —
(Astrid grabs at an air dream with her hands and then sets it free, sadly.)
But it seems that your —
Well it's — This —
Quite frankly Macy, the book is just not enticing enough
On its own To to to —

MACY: Not enticing enough to what?

ASTRID: Not enticing enough to make anyone want to read it.
(Pause.)

MACY: Oh
Not enticing enough to do that
(Pause: fork on plate, food back and forth back and forth, and then set down without a single bite.)

MACY: Well then
I guess this dinner is over

ASTRID: Macy
You haven't even touched — Look at this food:
This is beautiful food!
You never get to eat at Panet
This food will change your life / Enjoy enjoy my dear

MACY: Change your life Do you know
I
On the way here I
I wanted to walk across the bridge and the machines were broken
So some dreary clerk gave me a reading
And I had to wait for the results with all the Tradepacks
At the border crossing on the bridge
And I kept thinking
Or I thought
Life can be so — It's all just so— *(She looks up at Astrid.)*
Oh
Never mind

SANDY: Yes.

ANNE: You didn't have to answer so quickly. You could have thought about it a bit first.

SANDY: Why beat around the bush. Fed up with you. That's it. Just as I was fed up with Jim.

ANNE: But what was there to be fed up about?

(Sandy stares at Anne.)

ANNE: But we loved each other.

SANDY: I love profiteroles, but that doesn't mean . . .

ANNE: What's that?

SANDY: What?

ANNE: Profit something. What you just said.

SANDY: Profiteroles?

ANNE: Yeah, that.

SANDY: Pastry filled with cream.

ANNE: That sounds good.

SANDY: You usually pour chocolate syrup over them.

ANNE: Wow.

SANDY: Can I get back to . . .

ANNE: I'm sorry, but I always like to learn.

SANDY: But somehow we went from doomed marriages to profiteroles.

ANNE: You think they're doomed?

SANDY: Doomed, doomed, doomed. Kaput. Dead. They've passed on! These marriages are no more! They have ceased to be! They have expired and gone to meet their maker! They're a stiff! Bereft of life, they rest in peace! Their metabolic processes are now history. They are off the twig! They have kicked the bucket, shuffled off this mortal coil, run down the curtain and joined the choir invisible!! THESE ARE EX-MARRIAGES!! *(Pause.)* Did you recognize the Parrot Sketch from Monty Python? I love Monty Python, don't you.

ANNE: Not really, no.

SANDY: There's your problem.

ANNE: Not liking Monty Python?

SANDY: Having no sense of humor. There are times you are a stick in the mud, Anne.

ANNE: I am not.

SANDY: You are. A. Stick. In. The. Mud.

ANNE: And that's why Don left?

SANDY: I have no idea why Don left.

ANNE: So it might have been for other reasons.

SANDY: It might. But that doesn't mean you aren't a stick in . . .

ANNE: All right. I get it. The question is what to do now. I can't continue to live here in a hotel.

SANDY: Sure you can. It's on old Donny Wonny's credit card, isn't it?

ANNE: Oh, I can't . . .

SANDY: Oh, sure you can.

ANNE: You are a devil.

SANDY: Shall we order some food and drink.

SLASHER
Allison Moore

More information on this author may be found on the "Meet the Authors" web page at www.smithandkraus.com.

Seriocomic
Sheena, twenty-one
Hildy, fifteen
Frances, forty to fifty

> *Sheena, a pretty girl of average intelligence and an aspiring actress, is cast as the "last girl" in a low-budget slasher flick, which she thinks is the big break she's been waiting for. She intends to keep the news secret from her ultra-feminist angry mom, Frances, who has a questionable disability and gets around the house on a Rascal scooter. But Frances gets wind of Sheena's plans when the first assistant drops the script off at the house — unbeknownst to Sheena. Frances is prepared to do anything to stop Sheena from making the movie. Hildy is Sheena's little sister.*

> *(Frances's house. Hildy and Sheena step into the house holding their Cokes and the Sonic bag. Frances sits on her Rascal scooter, ready for battle. She holds the copy of the script.)*

FRANCES: You.

HILDY: Uh-oh.

SHEENA: What is that?

FRANCES: This? *(She rips a single page from the script.)*

SHEENA: Don't!

FRANCES: Oh, I thought you didn't know what it was.

SHEENA: Where did you get it?

FRANCES: I was actually hoping that you DIDN'T know —

SHEENA: Give it to me —

FRANCES: Because this, *this* is a chronicle of female degradation, one hundred and five pages in which a virginal young woman named "Sloan" is terrorized — *(Frances rips another page.)*

SHEENA: Mother!

FRANCES: *(And another.)* sexually objectified —

SHEENA: Stop!

FRANCES: *(And another.)* TORTURED AND RAPED AFTER BEING BATHED IN ANOTHER WOMAN'S BLOOD.

HILDY: Gross.

FRANCES: No, Hildy. "Gross" is a booger. "Gross" is vomit, or feces. *This* is a contagion in which the most reprehensible acts are packaged as entertainment — not just entertainment, but as TITILATION, so that men like Marc Hunter will continue to think that it's HOT to see women RAPED AND KILLED! I am going to track him down and cram every single page down his throat, page after page, until his dangly little uvula is castrated by a thousand paper cuts and he chokes on his own blood! Or maybe I'll just burn it.

(Sheena makes a quick grab for the script, but Frances zips away on her scooter. A chase.)

SHEENA: I won't let you!

FRANCES: Where are the matches!

SHEENA: I am doing this movie!

FRANCES: OVER MY DEAD BODY!

SHEENA: I can arrange that!

FRANCES: I will lock you in the closet before I let that happen! I will force-feed you the collected works of Betty Freidan! I will not allow you to be tortured and humiliated —

SHEENA: I WANT TO BE TORTURED, OK?

FRANCES: What did you just say.

SHEENA: I want to be tied up, and look scared and scream my head off, and you know why? BECAUSE IT'S A MOVIE.

FRANCES: I am not hearing this.

SHEENA: I AM IN A MOVIE! I'm the STAR! And I didn't just get the part! I NEGOTIATED! I demanded more money and I GOT IT! YOU'RE SUPPOSED TO BE PROUD OF ME!

FRANCES: — I'm supposed to be proud you want to be degraded?

SHEENA: IT'S NOT REAL, MOTHER! I'M IN CONTROL!

FRANCES: You're actually retarded, aren't you?

SHEENA: You know what? I'm outta here.

(Sheena bounds up the stairs, sound of drawers opening and closing. Frances comes to the foot of the stairs, talking up at Sheena.)

FRANCES: I always knew you weren't smart, but I didn't think you were actually STUPID. Have you learned NOTHING? Watching me bang my head on the glass ceiling, day after day —

(Sheena reappears at the top of the stairs.)

SHEENA: You haven't worked in years.

FRANCES: I HAVE CHRONIC FATIGUE!

SHEENA: You want to stop me from making this movie? Here's your chance: Come up here and stop me.

(An expectation.)

FRANCES: Don't mock me.

SHEENA: I dare you. Walk up these stairs and admit that there's nothing wrong with you, and MAYBE I won't do the movie.

HILDY: Sheena, what are you doing?

SHEENA: — The choice is yours, Mom.

HILDY: You know she can't go up stairs.

SHEENA: Oh yes she can. She just doesn't want to.

FRANCES: That's not true.

SHEENA: I want you to admit that you're a lazy, bitter drug addict —

HILDY: Sheena, stop it.

SHEENA: Who would rather rail about injustice than GET A JOB —

FRANCES: You're beyond cruel.

SHEENA: What's cruel is pretending you're too tired to even walk across a room, and forcing your daughter to support you so you can spend all your time screaming that you've been discriminated against.

FRANCES: I HAVE been discriminated against —

SHEENA: The city gave Marshall Davis that cleaning contract because you couldn't do the job.

FRANCES: I DID the job.

SHEENA: You took a whole day to clean one floor!

FRANCES: Hello! I'm DISABLED, of course it's going to take me longer.

SHEENA: You are such a victim! God! You talk about how people are so afraid of strong, powerful women "like you." But no one is afraid of you, and you know why? Because you don't DO ANYTHING! Ever since Dad left you've done nothing! Well I'm actually DOING something now, and you can't stop me.

(Sheena disappears onto the second floor.)

FRANCES: Oh, so this is your big statement? Well, I've got a question for you: Who controls the film? Who controls the money, huh? I'll give you a hint: it's not you! You and the rest of your generation, you're all too busy getting boob jobs and counting carbs to notice that WOMEN ARE STILL ROYALLY SCREWED. They pat you on the head, tell you discrimination is over. Who needs equal rights when you've got the WNBA? They trot out Condoleeza Rice once a month like she's the

EQUALITY BONG so you're all too stoned to notice that WE STILL ONLY MAKE SEVENTY-SIX CENTS ON THE DOLLAR!

(Sheena barrels down the stairs with a bag of clothes and climbs over Frances like she's a piece of furniture.)

SHEENA: Get out of my way. I am not going to let you — OW!

HILDY: Stop it!

FRANCES: You are NOT taking my car.

SHEENA: It's MY car, mom. I bought it after you totaled the last one ramming into Marshall Davis's Expedition!

HILDY: Where are you going?!

FRANCES: If you do this movie, I am disowning you, Sheena. I'll never speak to you again.

HILDY: Mom!

SHEENA: Fine.

HILDY: Sheena!

SHEENA: She's all yours.

HILDY: You can't leave. What am I supposed to do?!

SHEENA: You're the genius. Figure it out.

FRANCES: They've turned my own daughter against me.

SHEENA: No, you did that all on your own.

SOUL SAMURAI
Qui Nguyen

Comic
Sally, nineteen
Dewdrop, nineteen

> *Sally and Dewdrop, two rebellious nineteen-year-old girls, are going out
> for some illicit party supplies. Sally tries to calm Dewdrop's nerves about
> being in Bushwick, a particularly dangerous section of Brooklyn.*

SALLY: Flip the switch, bitch. This tired shit is bugging me out.

DEWDROP: Maybe we should head home, Sal. It's almost dark —

SALLY: What? You scared of the dark or somethin'?

DEWDROP: No.

SALLY: 'Cause I'm not. I like the dark.

DEWDROP: Get off me, whore.

SALLY: Then what's wrong, love?

DEWDROP: The radio just said —

SALLY: Correction, bitch. Radios can't "say" anything.

DEWDROP: What?

SALLY: Radios. They are incapable of speech. They project noise. Transmit fre-
quencies. Relay electromagnetic signals that our ears detect as sound.
But they cannot speak. Speaking is an attribute that infers cognitive and
sentient thought. Radios are not sentient so thusly speech is something
still outside their realm of capability. By using the expression, "The radio
just said," you personify the radio as something other than just a noise
box and that, my oriental love-bot, is dumb as a motherfucker.

DEWDROP: Bitch, are you stoned?

SALLY: I'm just correcting. If you're gonna hang with me, yella girl, you gotsa
speak proper.

DEWDROP: Whatevs.

SALLY: And secondly —

DEWDROP: Oh, there's a secondly?

SALLY: Of course there is, bitch. And, secondly, do you really believe that anyone is gonna arrest us? Here? In Brooknam? For someone to get arrested,
baby girl, someone has to be there to do the arresting. And do you hap-

pen to see any bacon bits sprinkled anywhere in this diverse salad bowl of Bushwick?

DEWDROP: Well . . .

SALLY: Now look hard. What does your eye spy?

DEWDROP: Nuthin'.

SALLY: Then shut your pretty little pie hole, 'cause you and me are on an adventure.

DEWDROP: For some pot?

SALLY: Oh, when you say it that way, it doesn't make it sound special.

DEWDROP: Couldn't we have just scored some from the stoners down the hall?

SALLY: Ew no. I'm not going anywhere near those two midwestern motherfuckers. Have you seen the way they look at us?

DEWDROP: No.

SALLY: They'd want hand jobs.

DEWDROP: All guys want hand jobs.

SALLY: Well, if you wanna whore yourself for some hash, that is your prerogative. Me, I want my icky wicky coming from somewhere respectable.

DEWDROP: Like Bushwick?

SALLY: Yo, the only people that find Bushwick scary is white folks.

DEWDROP: Um. You're white.

SALLY: Just on the outside.

DEWDROP: Is there any other way of being white?

SALLY: Look, yella girl, underneath this blandy Mandy exterior is a girl of much more cultural charisma and street know-how than some cracka from Connecticut.

DEWDROP: You are a cracker from Connecticut.

SALLY: But underneath —

DEWDROP: You're a honky. Sal, your family has two homes. One in Connecticut, the other in the fucking Hamptons. You spent every summer during your adolescence going to — what — tennis camp? And you're now attending one of the most expensive colleges in the nation without carrying a student loan. You're not just white — you're fucking glow-in-the-dark radioactive neon white. You're so white, standing next to you, I look like the night.

SALLY: Oh, but you're forgetting one thing.

(Sally stops the car and puts it in park.)

DEWDROP: And what's that?

SALLY: I'm a big ol' dyke who loves fucking brown girls. I think that'll keep me from voting Republican anytime soon.

SOUTHERN RAPTURE
Eric Coble
More information on this author may be found on the "Meet the Authors" web page at www.smithandkraus.com.

Dramatic
Marjorie, thirties to forties
Allissa, thirties to forties

> *Allissa is with a theater group that is putting on a production of* Rapture in America *(obviously, a doppelgänger for* Angels in America*), which has her local community in quite a tizzy. Marjorie wants them to cancel the play.*

MARJORIE: It is so great to see you, Allissa. It's been what, since the United Way gala —

ALLISSA: Yes.

MARJORIE: And little Annie's performance.

ALLISSA: Yes.

MARJORIE: She was adorable. Just adorable.

ALLISSA: She's certainly cute. But honestly the child can't carry a tune with both hands and a wagon.

MARJORIE: Oh, now —

ALLISSA: I'm her mother, I can say that. I found myself wishing they'd play the piano louder to drown her out. Or something She has so many many gifts, but I fear singin' is not among them.

MARJORIE: *(Still smiling.)* Well, it was a play by six-year-olds to kick off a charity event.

ALLISSA: Of course.

MARJORIE: You look terrific. Are you doing your hair differently.

ALLISSA: No.

MARJORIE: Maybe it's just the angle. Or my lack of sleep.

ALLISSA: How are rehearsals going?

MARJORIE: Super! Just super-duper! I mean, it's mammoth, just such an epic mammoth bear of a play, but my God, Allissa, you should see what the actors are doing, they are so committed, so *brave*!

ALLISSA: I guess they'd have to be. Or at least Mickey.

MARJORIE: Well, he's certainly got a daunting part —

ALLISSA: I'm concerned, Marjorie.

MARJORIE: Me too. What about?

ALLISSA: Our theater.

MARJORIE: Oh, that's so sweet of you. But we're fine, Allissa, we're great!

ALLISSA: When you first chose this play, I thought, "Well, bravo, that sounds like a very important play —"

MARJORIE: It is

ALLISSA: " — certainly it should be our company putting it on here."

MARJORIE: We should.

ALLISSA: But I did not read it. I trusted you

MARJORIE Absolutely, thank you.

ALLISSA: And now I'm concerned.

MARJORIE: Well, the good news is we're selling tickets like crazy, we've started a conversation in the community, we're really doing everything a theater should do.

ALLISSA: Does that include angering people?

MARJORIE: Yes. No! We're not trying to anger, we're engaging in dialogue, we're dialoguing with the black bear.

ALLISSA: Is that a theater term?

MARJORIE: Yes. Yes, it is. Isn't it fun to be on the inside?

ALLISSA: You seem particularly squirmy today, Marjorie.

MARJORIE: I'm not! I'm just excited! Actually, if you could just excuse me —

ALLISSA: I won't take but a moment. Here's my concern.

(Marjorie sits again, uncomfortably.)

ALLISSA: I am very very proud of our city. We truly are world class. And everyone knows a world-class city has an orchestra, a ballet company, an art museum, hopefully an opera, at least one major sports franchise, an international airport, and strong regional theater. We have all that, praise God. But I am very concerned that by producing this play, that you could be turning our citizens against the arts — all the arts, or at least public funding of the arts. There are many of us who have worked too long and too hard to suddenly find ourselves facing the world with our flies hanging open.

MARJORIE: Absolutely. And we have no intentions of leaving our flies open.

ALLISSA: *(Brandishing the newspaper.)* I find that hard to believe when you allow your actors to say that they adopt children and teach them about consensual male intercourse!

MARJORIE: OK, first, I think he was misquoted. 'Cause Mickey's never adopted anything. Children, puppies, kittens, nothing. Second, I can't control what my actors say. They're free citizens —

ALLISSA: But they represent the theater, they represent our city.

MARJORIE: Then God help our city.

ALLISSA: I want to be able to bring my mother to the theater, Marjorie. Honestly, I'd just like her to be able to read her newspaper again! These stories, these phrases — I've had to drive over to her house at six a.m. every day this week to get her paper before her and shred the offensive sections and then blame it on the poor Russell terrier next door and she hates that dog now, she is thinking of taking a beebee gun to an innocent dog because your theater is putting on this gay fantasia!

MARJORIE: I'm so sorry.

ALLISSA: I guess I don't understand what you think we'll get out of this?

MARJORIE: I think . . . this play says a lot about where people go wrong about self-acceptance and self-responsibility and what it truly means to be a great nation. And a great city. It's important.

ALLISSA: Well, aren't there other very important plays coming out from France and Russia and . . . China . . . you're not doing those.

MARJORIE: Because nobody here would understand them.

ALLISSA: My point exactly.

(Beat. They watch each other.)

ALLISSA: You don't have to do just funny light ha-ha plays. Your season closer last season — *Steel Magnolias* — I cried during that. I cried and I laughed and so did everyone else. Including my mother.

MARJORIE: And when we did *The Hairy Ape* — that was another dramatic one —

ALLISSA: Yes. I didn't care so much for that one. But that was nothing compared to this. I don't know that I can tell my neighbors to come see this one at all.

MARJORIE: I don't know if you can. But if they do, they're going to hear some amazing dialogue and get taken on such an intellectual and emotional and theatrical trip.

ALLISSA: So this is your definition of good theater.

MARJORIE: We'll see Friday.

WHAT ONCE WE FELT

Ann Marie Healy

More information on this author may be found on the "Meet the Authors" web page at www.smithandkraus.com.

Dramatic
Macy, thirty
Astrid, forty to sixty

> *Astrid, an "old school" literary agent, tries to convince Macy, an idealistic but misguided writer, to trade in her "fertility scan card" so that Claire Monsoon, media scion, can use it to have a baby. In return, Astrid explains, Claire will publish Macy's novel: "The last print published novel ever . . ." Macy refuses at first out of moral indignation and fear of getting arrested. As Astrid presses her, however, she realizes that this is her last chance at literary fame and glory. Ultimately, she decides to make the deal, and she and Astrid end the scene by celebrating the choice. (Note: A backslash [/] indicates where the next line of dialogue overlaps the current one.)*

MACY: OK
　　So / So?
ASTRID: So they read it
　　And they really love it
MACY: What does that mean?
ASTRID: They really love it means They really love it
　　They want to publish it You know
　　If if if /
　　Always if
MACY: If what?
　　They want to publish it or they will?
ASTRID: They want to /
　　If they want to badly enough
　　They will
MACY: There's a big difference You know in intention I've seen this sort of
　　Thing
　　Well you know that last / Time

ASTRID: Of course I know that last time We all know that last time / Macy all
    of us ALL OF US (Have heard about that last time)
MACY: Oh God did I talk about that
    Too much?
    I should shut up about that last time But they / you know they
ASTRID: I know I know
    But this time is not like that time They love this
MACY: And I'm willing to do some rewrites
    I know I've left things somewhat ambiguous
    So I'm open to discussing /
    The ambiguity
    (Not discussing the origin of it
    But discussing the idea of the origin of it — Or the idea of —
    Whatever)
ASTRID: Oh sure sure
    No no that wasn't up —
    Dear don't talk to yourself
    You sound insane
    When you do that don't do that Macy please
    Now the rewrites weren't up for debate / They just said
MACY: Was something else up for debate?
    Astrid?
    Astrid?
ASTRID: No no
    They love it / They love it
MACY: They want to publish it Or they will? /
    Astrid?
ASTRID: They want to
    And they will
    There is a different item / Up for debate but it's
    Negli—
MACY: So they want to
    But we don't know if they will (Just like last time)
ASTRID: It's just a small thing
    And we don't need to talk about it now
    For now let's celebrate
    We'll have that duck peach melba
    Dusty Whatever Dish
    And I will get good and drunk /

And tell you far too many juicy tales of —

MACY: I don't want to celebrate No no Astrid

I want you to tell me —

ASTRID: Look at this

Fruity spiky thing / In my drink

MACY: What is the item up for debate?

ASTRID: Did you see this

Did you see this thing? / Is this a kumquat?

MACY: What is the item up for debate

Tell me

ASTRID: They have a favor That's all

It's not the /

It's not

MACY: A favor!

I wrote a novel!

Why don't they do me a —

ASTRID: I offered them something in exchange

For publishing your novel /

It's not a big deal

MACY: !I thought that in exchange for publishing my novel

!They got to read my novel in its published form

!Exchange!?

!Exchange!?

(*Astrid inspects her for a moment and takes a sip of her drink. It is possible, from the look on Astrid's face, that some of the other Panet patrons have overheard Macy's outburst.*)

ASTRID: My dear You may think it is all the rage to express

Ta passion

But the rest of us —

Your elders —

We are not impressed.

You might do well to tuck that temperament away

Not the Bright Young Thing you once were

Are you?

MACY: !But I believe!

!I know!

!I deserve better — !

ASTRID: You want to know what really happened last time?

This is what happened last time:

(Gesturing toward Macy's passionate display of emotion) This
We were minutes away from signing the deal and then they saw you —
(Vague gesture for Macy's temper.)
And then we lost —
(Vague gesture for "the whole deal.")
And now we're what?
What are we now?

MACY: !Now we're —
!We're —
!We're —

ASTRID: *(Displays of patience and a scan around the room.)* Now we're not any-
thing my dear
Now we are reserved We are friendly to all But we are reserved.
The refined reserve Macy
Is the "little black dress" of publishing.
It is always appropriate. It is always en vogue. A refined reserve
Will placate all
And
It will compliment my flamboyance perfectly! *(Motioning to her drink
and taking a big gulp.)* Yes! It is indeed a kumquat!
(Slight pause.)
Comprends ma cherie?

MACY: Yes
I understand.
A refined reserve
I get it.
(A little pause to start the conversation again.)
What what is the item up for debate?

ASTRID: The publisher
Claire Monsoon
You remember / her?

MACY: !Oh no Claire Monsoon?!
!Terrible taste!
!In books! In life! /
!Claire! Oh God a favor for her?!

ASTRID: Shhhhhhhhhhh Just listen
SHT!

MACY: I'm listening Sorry
Refined reserve / Listening

ASTRID: Because you don't even want kids Anyway /
      You said so yourself
MACY: Kids?
      What do kids have to / Do with this?
ASTRID: She
      Claire
      You know
      She likes the novel
      But it's literary and
      You know how they are about literary these days But they like it /
      They said so
MACY: You said they loved it Not liked it but loved it
ASTRID: She does love it
      But Claire takes convincing
      I have to serve up my secret Astrid sauce— You know she just wants
      Trash
      She wants oh
      You know
      She wants all self-help
      All the time
      She wants fast and cheap digital downloads
      Or else she wants Inspector Ovid
      And his stupid talking dog
      Oh my God will they ever stop pushing that inane Inspector Ovid on
      us? So I just
      You know
      I threw something more enticing into the mix
MACY: More enticing than the actual novel? Enticing as in?
      (Macy tries to restrain herself.)
      Enticing as in what?
ASTRID: Enticing as in —
      (Inspecting her food.)
      Enticing as in —
      Well without me throwing a little extra into the mix —
      Let's face it Macy:
      The most you might have hoped for was was was
      A few hundred digital downloads on some godforsaken hard drive who
      knows where
      No pizzazz

I'm boring
I'm boring myself

ASTRID: *(Pulling a kumquat out and eating it with her fingers.)* You really
should try one
They're stuffed full of liquor
Like sucking a shot from a wet sock!

MACY: What did you offer Claire to entice her?

ASTRID: I shouldn't have
It was ahem
A very unconventional contingency / I shouldn't have even tried

MACY: What did you offer her?
(Pause.)

ASTRID: Claire mentioned to me that she —
She's in a bit of a sticky situation with the RSS —
That is —
Well she would like to download a baby but —
She can't, you see
She just — She can't

MACY: I don't understand Why can't she?

ASTRID: Because she —
Well —
It —
You know —
She doesn't have the right scan card

MACY: !Wait! !Wait! !Claire Monsoon is a!
Tradepack!?

ASTRID: *(Looking around Panet to see if anyone heard that.)* Would you please
keep your voice down Please

MACY: *(Lowered voice.)* Claire Monsoon is a (Tradepack)?

ASTRID: I don't know
She didn't say as much to me but —
Yes: It seems that Claire Monsoon is a *(Whisper.)* Tradepack
People used to be able to slip through the RSS
In the very early stages of The Transition
It used to be much more common
Wealthy people —
Powerful —
Someone like Claire Monsoon —

She probably paid off some bureaucrat at RSS
To keep it quiet
I've heard some people do that
So —
MACY: Claire Monsoon is a
Wow Wow I never would have
Wow
ASTRID: When The Transition started
You know
They didn't have us all sequenced and added to the system
Not like now
It was totally chaotic back then
The whole thing
Chaotic, yes, but at least we could breathe a bit
Sigh:
Not like now
Now we have fully organized and expedited our own Nadir —
!But I digress ma cherie!
MACY: Wow
So
So wait
So what was the item up for debate?
Astrid?
ASTRID: I wanted to entice her to do one last great novel in print
Before they shut down all the presses
And toss out all the pulp
Not just some Self-Help Lipstick Stomach Staple Who Ha
But a real gesture towards literature!
A very special work of "biting satire and dystopian leanings"
An exquisite, gold-embossed trim, first edition, print published novel
that goes by the name of:
ASTRID/MACY: *Terror's Peon*
ASTRID: *(She tries to breeze through this next section.)* So I told her if she would
publish *Terror's Peon* in print
You might *(Vague gesture for "loan.")* her your scan card
Just for a few months
MACY: I might what?
ASTRID: She wants to use your Keeper card

To download a baby
She can't download with a Tradepack card, of course / So
MACY: Wait
!I might what?!
ASTRID: Loan her You might loan her your scan / card
MACY: Loan her?!
Loan her!
What?
That's not not not
She shouldn't even
And what did she say?
What could she possibly say / to that offer?
ASTRID: Yes
MACY: What?
What did she say?
ASTRID: Yes
She said yes
She said she would publish it
In print
Full slot
The last print published novel
Ever
Terror's Peon
Over 500,000 copies in the initial printing
But that's just the first run
She wants to make it look like one last farewell to fiction
Grand fanfare all that
Every airport on the planet will carry you
The big shakes before you know
She goes back to her Inspector Ovid and the talking dog trash
If you would
Just your card for a few months
No one will ever even know it's you
No one will ever know anything at all
They'll all think she's having her baby
Just like any other Keeper
She's afraid to ask, you see
She can't ask anyone at work

Or any friends
If anyone knew
Or found out
(Astrid takes in Macy's face.)
ASTRID: I'm sorry
It was wrong of me
I know you young ladies only get one download
But you said you didn't care for children
I didn't think it would matter
If you gave your download to / To To To
MACY: I don't care about my download !My download?
That's the last —
I care about —
My life —
My life outside of incarceration — My
My
They execute women for this
That's what I've heard
The RSS has
In the North
In those weird little mountain towns
With the fucked-up goats
They do
I've heard stories
If I went up for trial
In the North
I could be executed in some weird little mountain town
With a line of fucked-up goats Looking me in the eyes while I died
Alone
I would die
Alone
With the goats
Or
Or
!Why would I fuck with the RSS! This is the RSS
This is not your grandmother baking soda bread and handing you a long
tall glass of milk This is the RSS
The R-S-S
These women are MOTHERFUCKERS —

ASTRID: *(Clucking.)* Is this just you or is this —

MACY: What?

ASTRID: Is this just you or is this generational? This this behavior.

First of all, keep your voice down please. Do I need to remind you:

We are in a public place Macy.

Not just a public place but the public place: Panet

You do not shout out *(A whisper.)* motherfucker at Panet

Honestly

Who raised you girls?

You young girls were raised in a school of barracudas

What happened to manners and

Tsk tsk

Sit up straight

Posture please my dear

Sit up straight

Using knives and forks and small sips

Swish the water in your mouth

Don't gulp

Mastication please mastication

All right

Let's discuss the issue at hand

Like ladies

Yes?

OK?

MACY: Yes

OK

ASTRID: OK

Ladies?

MACY: Ladies yes Ladies

ASTRID: Now

This is not about mountain goats

This is not even about the RSS

This is about your book:

Who will read your book

If your book is never published Eh?

This is a simple contractual arrangement

You won't go to trial

You won't be put in prison You are simply

This is simply

A business proposal

MACY: Loaning Claire Monsoon

My scan card

Has nothing to do with the business

Or the craft

Or the whatever

Of writing a novel

ASTRID: So you say Duly noted

(Astrid takes a moment to chomp on her kumquat drink.)

She's just one woman Macy

She's just one woman and she wants to download a baby

Perhaps she's an imperfect mother

According to the RSS

Perhaps

But

(A gesture for "is this so bad?")

At my age, I find perfection overrated

(Another look around Panet and a smile and nod at someone in the distance.)

We used to joke about the RSS

When I was younger

They were They were Ham-fisted Without a Jot of Humor

They were women with bad breath

And mullet-headed haircuts

Anyway

It was selfish on my part

To have ever suggested this

So

(She waves her arms in a vague gesture.)

Let's eat and

Just forget the whole thing

Eat eat!

Those short ribs are positively sweating with delicious shivers!

You must eat!

(Pause. They eat in silence.)

MACY: The last print published novel Ever

ASTRID: Ever yes ever

Farewell to Fiction!

No more
I hope you like Inspector Ovid
They put his talking dog to sleep in Series Seven
And then a canine angel comes to save the day

MACY: Right well

ASTRID: Eat eat
Oh look there's Vivien LeFray
She's working with Claire on that DNA diet scheme
One of those Digi-Direct Downloads
(A wave and then a sigh.)
Seven secrets to something something
(They both eat quietly.)

MACY: That clerk /
I keep thinking of her face

ASTRID: What clerk

MACY: That woman
That Tradepack
In the
Never mind
(To herself.) Change your life

ASTRID: Hmmmmmmmm
I think our waitress might be a Keeper
Don't you?
Did you see her hands?
So long and lean
Total Keeper hands
They must be running out of Tradepacks
For the service sector
Did you hear that?
Didn't someone say that? Macy?

MACY: What?

ASTRID: I lost you for a moment
(This peach melba dust tastes like it came from a Powder / mix)

MACY: How can I be sure that no one would ever find out?

ASTRID: This is Claire Monsoon we're talking about here Claire Monsoon has
her ducks in a row

MACY: Yes
OK yes
Sure Yes

ASTRID: Yes
  She has her ducks in a row?
MACY: Yes
  I said
  Yes
  She can use my scan card
  Yes
  (Pause.)
ASTRID: All right
  Well then
  Congratulations This novel
  This novel is / She loves it
MACY: As long as she loves it
  And she can get other people to love it
  Then the rest is
  The rest is *(Vague gesture for "incidental.")*
  (Macy pulls out the scan card and slides it to Astrid.) Take it
  Just take it and put it away and
  And let's
  I want one of those
  With the kumquat
  Get me one of those /
  Immediately
ASTRID: Absolutely
  Oh and
  This goes without saying
  I trust you will utilize
  That refined reserve
  When you go in to speak with them No one can
  You realize
  No one can ever know
  Any of the details.
MACY: Are you fucking kidding me?
  Of course I'll be reserved
  I'll be impenetrable
  As long as they publish my novel
  I will be the cipher of Perseus Publishing

ASTRID: Well then
   (She raises her pink drink in a cheer.) Cheers to you Macy
   Cheers to your creation
MACY: Phhhhhew
   Anything
   Anything to bring this thing out into the world

WHY TORTURE IS WRONG, AND THE PEOPLE WHO LOVE THEM
Christopher Durang

Comic
Felicity, late twenties to early thirties
Zamir, late twenties to midthirties

> *Felicity, an attractive, smart young woman, wakes up in a motel and discovers she is in bed with a sleeping man, Zamir, who she has no recollection of even meeting. This isn't the sort of the thing that usually happens to her, though she may have gone out the night before to relax and have a drink. Zamir, who is probably Middle Eastern but could be Italian or Greek, wakes up friendly and chatty. There is something both appealing and scary about him. Felicity starts out polite and a touch embarrassed, but as their conversation goes on, she becomes alarmed — though the scene remains predominantly comic.*

> *(A bedroom in a motel. A man and woman asleep in bed. Man is in underwear and T-shirt [or shirtless] and has dark hair. Woman in slip or maybe bra and panties, or wrapped in a towel. Her name is Felicity. Felicity wakes first. Wakes up startled. She has NO IDEA where she is. Looks over at the man; he's still asleep. She gasps — she has no idea who he is. She peers closer — no, no idea. She decides to quietly sneak out of the room. Finds a dress, starts to put it on.)*

MAN: Hey, how'd you sleep?

FELICITY: Fine. Thank you.

MAN: I was so drunk!

FELICITY: Really. That's too bad. How do you feel now?

MAN: My head hurts, but I'm used to that.

FELICITY: Uh-huh. Was . . . was I drunk too?

MAN: Were you drunk too??? *(Laughs.)*

FELICITY: Yes, that's my question.

MAN: Oh, well I'm just repeating it because . . . wow . . . you were SO drunk. I mean "apocalypse now" kind of drunk. You were dancin' like crazy, then you'd throw up, then you'd dance like crazy, and you'd throw up again. It was . . . kinda hot.

FELICITY: *(Baffled why it's hot.)* Really?

MAN: Well, not the vomit. I may have my kinky side — as you know.

(He looks at her knowingly; she looks blank, and worried.)

MAN: But it doesn't include regurgitation. I just meant the crazy abandon of it. That's what was hot.

FELICITY: I see. Well, I'm glad you had a good time. Maybe we'll do it again some day. Do you know where my shoes are? I really should be going.

MAN: Going? I mean . . . going?

FELICITY: Well, I have a feeling I may have appointments. My brain isn't working yet, but I think I should get to my apartment.

MAN: Well, usually married people live together, no?

(She stares at him.)

FELICITY: What do you mean?

MAN: I'm just saying normally married people live together.

FELICITY: *(Screams.)* AAAAAAAAAAGGGGGHHHH.

MAN: What's the matter?

FELICITY: Are you saying we got married last night?

MAN: Yeah. In between all the vomiting. You said you never put out unless you got married first. And I thought you were joking, but I decided to call your bluff. And we got married. See . . . . *(He shows her a ring on his finger.)*

FELICITY: Oh my God. *(Looks at her hand.)* But I don't have a ring.

MAN: We got mugged on the way into the hotel.

FELICITY: Were we hurt?

MAN: I don't remember. I think you need to call and stop your credit cards though.

FELICITY: You mean my bag is gone?

MAN: Yeah, that's what I mean.

FELICITY: Did they take *your* credit cards?

MAN: I don't have any. I'm . . . footloose and fancy free.

FELICITY: Uh-huh. And you don't have any credit cards?

MAN: I don't have good credit. I don't like to pay bills. Plus I think food and electricity and housing should be free.

FELICITY: Do you have a job?

MAN: Um . . . well depends what you mean by a job.

FELICITY: I mean do you work and get paid?

MAN: I'm not sure what you mean.

FELICITY: Good God if we're married, do you have any money? Do I have to earn everything?

MAN: It would be great if you earned everything. I should have asked you last night, but thanks for offering it now.

FELICITY: I'm not offering it, I'm just trying to figure out . . .

MAN: Hey. I do stuff. Sometimes I drive a big van in the middle of the night, and I deliver things, and I get paid. Or I get a tip from someone where I can . . . you know score something big. And sometimes I just find money . . . under a rock, you know.

FELICITY: Under a rock?

MAN: Yeah I do something for somebody, it's a little dangerous, maybe a little illegal; and they tell me to go to some field and look for a tree by a rock, and underneath the rock there's this envelope with like, you know, a lotta cash.

FELICITY: Oh I'm feeling scared. Am I an alcoholic? Did I have a blackout? Did you give me a date rape drug?

MAN: You mean like penicillin?

FELICITY: No, I mean roofies or something.

MAN: Roofies. *(Laughs.)* Baby, I don't need to give anybody roofies to go to bed with them.

FELICITY: Well . . . is there . . . paperwork on this marriage?

MAN: I think so. Hold on.

FELICITY: If only I'm dreaming, and I can wake up.

MAN: That's a hurtful thing to say. I have a temper, you know, be careful. *(Goes through a pile of his clothes, finds something underneath.)* Here it is. *(Hands her something folder-like.)*

FELICITY: *(Takes it.)* It's a menu.

MAN: Yeah, the marriage certificate is inside.

FELICITY: *(She opens it.)* Ah. So it is.

MAN: See. I told you.

FELICITY: *(Looks at menu.)* Did we get married at Hooters?

MAN: No. That's where you threw up the first time. But Hooters told us of this minister guy who also makes porno. And he married us.

FELICITY: Also makes porno. I've never met anyone who makes porno.

MAN: Yeah, that's what you said last night. I hope you're not going to repeat yourself a lot in our marriage. That would be a drag.

FELICITY: Well it's obvious we should get this annulled.
(Man darkens, gets really mad.)

MAN: *(Vicious scary.)* Who the fuck do you think you're talking to? Get this annulled? You think I'm a refrigerator you can just send back to Sears?

FELICITY: Refrigerator?

MAN: I may have been drunk, but I gave a lot of thought to asking you to marry me. I've never been married. I said to myself, Zamir, it's about time you got married. *(To her again.)* You said you liked me last night, don't "dis" me by sayin' you want an annulment. I mean, do you wanna keep your teeth? You want your lungs to keep workin'?

FELICITY: Oh my God. OK, I see your point, don't get angry. And what about Zamir? Is your name Zamir?

ZAMIR: Yeah. It's Irish.

FELICITY: *(Choosing not to argue.)* OK. Oh my. You see, I just don't remember last night, not the marriage, not the sex, assuming there was sex, and of the sex I don't remember, I don't remember anything that was kinky. How do you define kinky?

ZAMIR: Oh baby, I'll define it for you again tonight.

FELICITY: I mean I don't know if you mean slightly kinky or truly disgusting.

ZAMIR: Oh, baby, talk dirty to me.

FELICITY: Look, I don't even remember meeting you. I really think we should get an annulment.

(He makes angry sound and motion.)

FELICITY: Or what about a trial separation?

ZAMIR: God you're making it worse and worse. I should tell you, my male ego is fragile, and when it gets bruised, I can get violent. It's a flaw in my character, but all the women in my family are dead.

FELICITY: What?

ZAMIR: No, they're not dead. But they can tell you, I can get violent. Definitely don't use your good china at dinner with me.

FELICITY: OK thanks for the tip.

ZAMIR: When can I meet your parents?

FELICITY: Um. How about never? Is never good for you?

(He looks violent.)

FELICITY: No, I'm kidding. How about . . . this afternoon? I'll call them right up.

ZAMIR: Oh, that's the gal I married. Give me a kiss.

(He squeezes her to him, kisses her.)

FELICITY: We should really brush our teeth.

ZAMIR: Ooooooh, kinky.

(She looks confused.)

Rights and Permissions

IMPORTANT NOTE: The complete text of every play in this volume is available from the performance rights holder, except as otherwise noted.

MONOLOGUES

ALL ABOARD THE MARRIAGE HEARSE © 2008 by Matt Morillo. Reprinted by permission of the author. For performance rights, contact Samuel French, 45 W. 25th St., New York, NY 10010 (www.samuel french.com) (212-206-8990).

THE AMISH PROJECT © 2009 by Jessica Dickey. Reprinted by permission of Morgan Jenness, Abrams Artists Agency. For performance rights, contact Samuel French, 45 W. 25th St., New York, NY 10010 (www .samuelfrench.com) (212-206-8990).

AND SOPHIE COMES TOO © 2005 by Meryl Cohn. Reprinted by permission of the author. For performance rights, contact Meryl Cohn (msbehavior@aol.com).

BARRIO HOLLYWOOD © 2008 by Elaine Romero. Reprinted by permission of Brue Ostler, Bret Adams Ltd. For performance rights, contact Samuel French, 45 W. 25th St., New York, NY 10010 (www.samuel french.com) (212-206-8990).

BEAUTY ON THE VINE © 2008 by Zak Berkman. Reprinted by permission of Olivier Sultan, Creative Artists Agency. For performance rights, contact Dramatists Play Service, 440 Park Ave. S., New York, NY 10016 (www.dramatists.com) (212-683-8960).

BLACK FOREST © 2008 by Anthony Giardina. Reprinted by permission of Bruce Ostler, Bret Adams Ltd. For performance rights, contact Broadway Play Publishing, 56 E. 81st St., New York, NY 10021 (www.broad-wayplaypubl.com) (212-772-8334).

CARTOON © 2008 by Steve Yockey. Reprinted by permission of the author. For performance rights, contact Samuel French, 45 W. 25th St., New York, NY 10010 (www.samuelfrench.com) (212-206-8990).

THE COLUMBINE PROJECT © 2009 by Paul Storiale. Reprinted by permission of the author. For performance rights, contact Paul Storiale (pstoriale@gmail.com).

DEAD MAN'S CELL PHONE © 2008 by Sarah Ruhl. Reprinted by permission of Bruce Ostler, Bret Adams Ltd. For performance rights,

SCENES